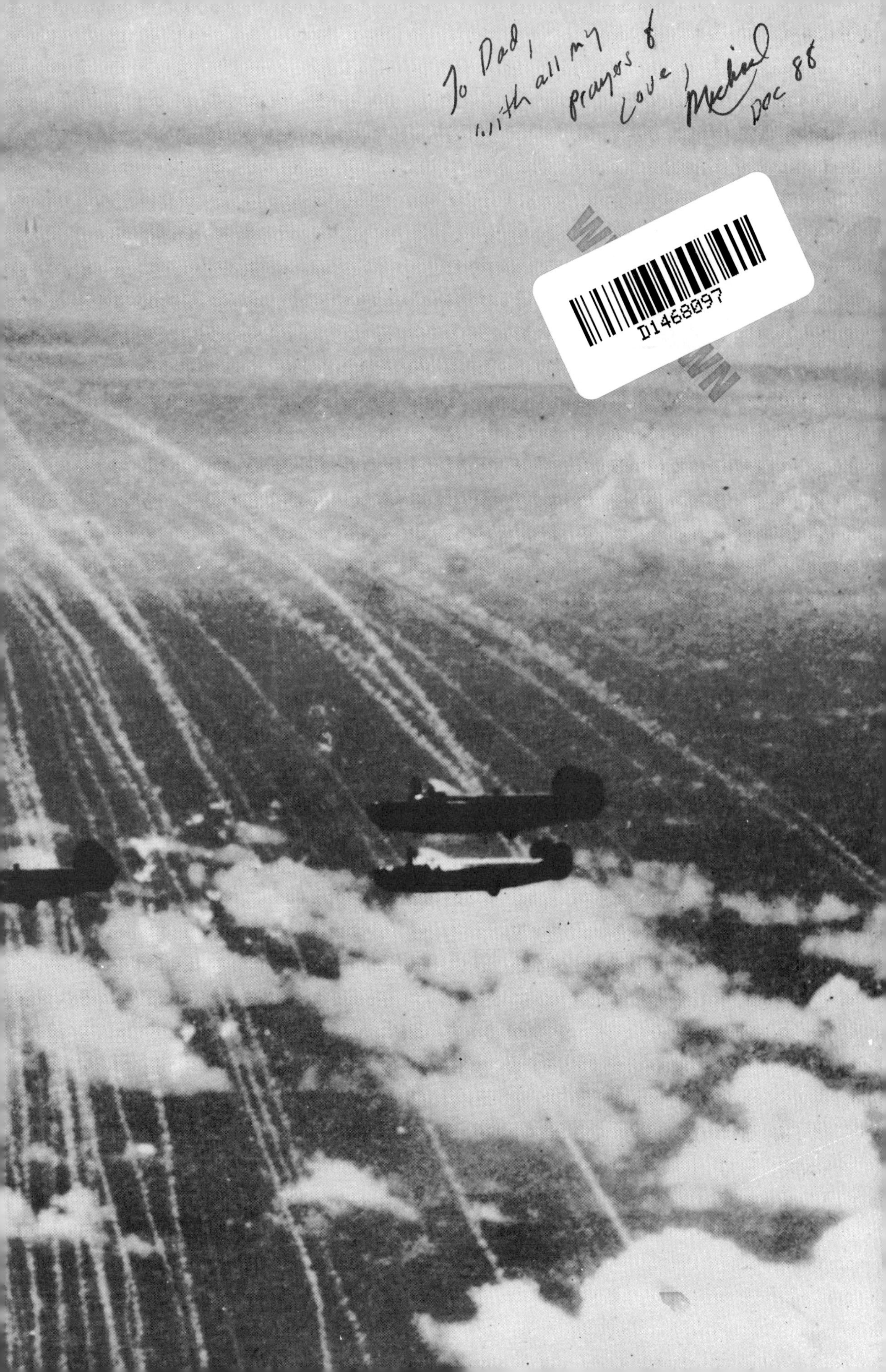

To Dad, with all my prayers & Love, Michael Dec 88

WAR IN THE PACIFIC

John Winton

Contents

WAR IN THE
PACIFIC
Pearl Harbor to Tokyo Bay

MAYFLOWER BOOKS, INC.,
575 LEXINGTON AVENUE,
NEW YORK CITY 10022.

Copyright © 1978 by
John Winton and
Sidgwick and Jackson Limited

Designed by Paul Watkins
Picture research by
Anne Horton
Map by Richard Natkiel

Right: The Far Eastern
war theatre
Front endpaper: Consolidated
B-24 Liberators escape
Japanese phosphorous bombs
over Iwo Jima
Back endpaper:
New Zealand troops unloading
equipment after Allied
landing on Green Islands in
the Solomons
Page 1: Japanese Marines in
Manila, 1941, and US
Marines in Iwo Jima, 1945
Pages 2/3: Japanese bomber
crashing off Okinawa

Map labels:

RUSSIA

MONGOLIA

C H I N A

PEKING

NANKIN
HANKOW

SHANGH

CHUNGKING
Hwang Ho
Yangtze kiang

AFGHANISTAN

DELHI

NEPAL

KARACHI

Ganges

IMPHAL

Burma Road
KUNMING
LASHIO
MANDALAY
HANOI
HAIPHONG

SWATOW
AMOY
CANTON

HONG KO

INDIA

CALCUTTA

BOMBAY
VIZAGAPATAM

BURMA

RANGOON

THAI-
LAND

BANGKOK

FRENCH
INDO-CHINA

SAIGON

HAINAN Luzon

CORREGIDOR

MANIL

MADRAS

BAY OF BENGAL

ANDAMAN
IS

SOUTH CHINA
SEA

TRINCOMALEE

COLOMBO
Ceylon

NICOBAR
IS

PENANG

SINGORA
KOTA BHARU

N BORNEO
BRUNEI
SARAWAK

Maldive
Is

Equator

ADDU
ATOLL

MALAYA

SINGAPORE

Borneo

Sumatra

DUTCH EA
JAVA SEA

Macassar St

**South-East Asia
Command** (Mountbatten)

BATAVIA
TJILATJAP Java

I N D I A N

O C E A N

COCOS IS

0   MILES   500
0   KM   800

SANSAPOR
BIAK I

HOLLANDIA

ADMIRALTY IS.

Bismarck Sea

N-E NEW
GUINEA

NEW IRELAND

RABAUL

BOUGAINVILLE

SOLOMON
ISLANDS

PERTH

DUTCH
NEW GUINEA

WEWAK

C. Gloucester

NEW
BRITAIN

NEW GEORGIA

A

SAIDOR
LAE

FINSCHHAFEN

Vella
Lavella

The Slot

Savo I

PAPUA

Nassau Bay

BUNA

Tulagi

Tassafaronga

SAN CRISTOBAL

PORT
MORESBY

Milne B.

GUADALCANAL

LOUISIADE
ARCH.

AUSTRALIA

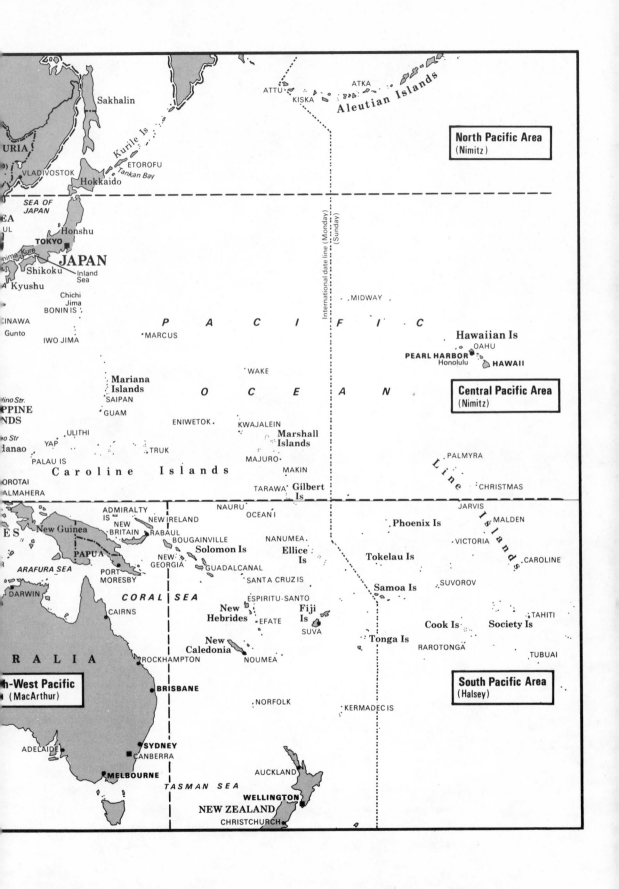

Pearl Harbor—the Stars and
Stripes still flying

1 PEARL HARBOR

'Let us pray that peace be now restored to the world and that God will preserve it always. These proceedings are now closed.'

With those words, General Douglas MacArthur, Supreme Allied Commander, brought to an end the ceremony of the signing of the Japanese surrender documents on board the U.S. battleship *Missouri* in Tokyo Bay on 2 September 1945.

All around the General, as he spoke, lay the symbols and elements of Allied power which had wrought victory from defeat. The General himself, as Commander-in-Chief, Southwest Pacific Area, had led an Allied advance from Australia to the Philippines. Next to him was Fleet Admiral Chester W. Nimitz, Commander-in-Chief, Pacific, who had commanded the great Allied drive across the Central Pacific, from the Gilbert Islands to Tokyo Bay. Also present were representatives of the other Allies: Great Britain, Australia, Canada, New Zealand, China, France, the Netherlands and Russia. Admirals Halsey and Spruance were there, representing the United States Navy, and in particular the Fast Carrier Task Force, which had been the spearhead of the Allied offensive. General Curtis LeMay, whose B-29 Superfortresses had bombed and burned most of Japan's major cities to rubble, and Admiral Lockwood, whose fast patrol submarines had torn the heart and bottom out of Japan's merchant fleet were there. There, too, were General Percival, who had surrendered Singapore, and General Jonathan Wainwright, of the Philippines, both now triumphantly released from prison camp. In the watching crowd were many other naval, army and air force officers and men, members of the press and the diplomatic

corps. Tokyo Bay in every direction was filled with grey warships, while over the distant horizon the most powerful fleet in naval history still kept the seas, watching for last-minute treachery. Overhead roared rank after rank, squadron after squadron, of Allied aircraft. Last, there were the political and military representatives of the defeated Japanese. Japan was the only nation in history to surrender unconditionally without one single foreign soldier ever setting foot on her metropolitan soil.

The Japanese surrender ceremony on board U.S.S. *Missouri,* 2 September 1945

The signing was a solemn moment. The silence was complete, wrote Admiral Sir Bruce Fraser, representing Great Britain, in his official report, 'except for the whirring and clicking of cameras and one could feel that all present at that gathering were struggling to adjust themselves mentally to the fact that they were witnessing the act which put an end to a long and bitter war.'[1] It all seemed a long time and a long way from a certain Sunday morning, early in December 1941, when Admiral Husband E. Kimmel, C.-in-C. Pacific, had looked out of his office window across the waters of Pearl Harbor to Ford Island and seen a swarm of Japanese planes bombing, torpedoing and strafing his battle fleet moored in Battleship Row. A spent 0.50 calibre bullet from one of those aircraft had actually broken a window pane and hit Kimmel on the chest. 'Too bad it didn't kill me,' he said to Nimitz, the man who had come to relieve him.

A great many people have been very wise very long after the event about Pearl Harbor and much of the latter-day wisdom has been at Admiral Kimmel's expense. Kimmel, like everybody else, was caught up in the swirl of one of the most climactic events of the war and one which contained a number of cruel paradoxes. The Japanese had longed for victory, and trained hard for it. Pearl Harbor put victory out of their reach. It was a victory which ensured their defeat. The Americans abhorred war and their politicians avoided it by every possible means, thus making it inevitable. Militarily, the attack was a disaster, but politically it came as a relief. For the Americans, it was a defeat which motivated their victory. Senior American officers who had drilled intensely for war were utterly overthrown by one of war's first weapons—surprise. Senior Japanese officers who had planned a brilliantly bold concept were then robbed of their deserved result by a cautious fleet commander.

The attack on Pearl Harbor, or something like it, had been looming for over a decade, ever since Japan began a campaign of territorial expansion with aggressive acts in Manchuria in 1931. Sooner or later, Japanese ambitions were bound to offend American moral scruples and commercial interests. Pre-war naval staff college appreciations, done by Nimitz and others, showed quite clearly that Japan was always the likeliest opponent. However, for years, treaty obligations abroad and a vocal isolationist minority at home kept America neutral, even under provocation. Even when the U.S. gunboat *Panay* was bombed and sunk in the Yangtse river and her survivors machine-gunned in December 1937, the United States accepted Japan's apology for an 'unfortunate mistake'. In the same year the Naval Limitation Treaty expired and Japan was free to build what warships she liked; she did so, concentrating upon aircraft carriers and laying down the keels of two giant 18.1-inch gun battleships *Yamato* and *Musashi*.

In July 1937 the Japanese manufactured a pretext for an undeclared war in China and the procession of military and political events which led to Pearl Harbor began to accelerate. By July 1939 Japanese forces occupied the whole Chinese coast, and on the 26th President Roosevelt gave the required six months' notice of abrogation of the 1911 Treaty of Commerce with Japan. The treaty lapsed on 26 January 1940 and Japanese imports of aircraft and aircraft spares, aviation fuel, lubricating oil, iron and steel raw material were, one by one, banned. In August 1940 the Japanese made the French Vichy government agree to their occupation of northern Indochina and in September signed a Tripartite defensive pact with Germany and Italy. Nobody could now have any doubts that Japan meant war, but the United States was still held in a neutral, isolationist stance.

Japan already had a plan for total war in the Far East, to capture the rich oil and mineral resources of the East Indies by invasions of Sumatra, Java, Thailand and Malaya. American air forces in the Philippines would be knocked out by carrier air

Above: Admiral Isoruku Yamamoto
Left: Admiral Chuichi Nagumo

Opposite: Before Pearl [...]
—Zekes warming up a[...]
taking off (centre) a[...]
of their carriers

attacks, and the islands would [...]
coming to the rescue, would be [...]
submarine from the Marshall a[...]
grâce would be applied in a grea[...]

This was an admirable plan a[...]
Japan had six fleet aircraft car[...]
in the East in the Mitsubishi Z[...]
trained in the skies over China. [...]
Fleet Air Arm attack on the Ita[...]
1940, and the earlier sinking of the German cruiser *Königsberg*
by British dive-bombers at Bergen in April 1940; they had an
excellent fleet torpedo-bomber, the Nakajima B5N 'Kate', and
an equally good fleet dive-bomber, the Aichi D3A 'Val'. An
encounter in the Philippine Sea might have gone hard for the
U.S. fleet.

However, it was possible that the Japanese main fleet might be
absent from the area, in support of the army, when the U.S. fleet
arrived. In January 1941 the C.-in-C. of the Japanese Combined
Fleet, Admiral Isoruku Yamamoto, began to think over the
possibilities of a pre-emptive strike against the U.S. fleet at its
main Pacific base at Hawaii. 'Strike first, declare war later' had
worked well against Russia and China. Commander Minoru
Genda, one of Japan's most experienced naval pilots, was ordered
to study the feasibility of such a plan. Genda reported in May
1941: the plan would work, if all six fleet carriers were used and
the great assault, which would have to be launched across 3,400
miles of ocean, was kept absolutely secret. Yamamoto was convinced, although many others, including Admiral Osami Nagano,
Chief of the Naval General Staff, were not. Urged on by
Yamamoto, training began. War games were held in August 1941.
In September, design and testing began on a special aerial
torpedo which could be dropped from a height and gain its
running depth quickly. The fleet went to sea for exhaustive
training in the realistic sea conditions and bad weather of the
North Pacific. An island in Kagoshima Bay, Kyushu, was used as
a target-substitute for Oahu. A scale model of Pearl Harbor was
built on the *Akagi*, the flagship of Vice-Admiral Chuichi
Nagumo, C.-in-C. of the 1st Air Fleet, in October and the first
crews briefed on the nature of their astounding mission. On 1
November Yamamoto was able to announce a possible day for
the strike—8 December. Two days later, Nagano withdrew his
opposition. The great gamble was on.

By this time, November 1941, the last days of peace were
running out. In April Japan had signed a non-aggression pact
with Russia, allowing her to withdraw some of her troops from
Manchuria. In July Vichy France agreed to a joint protectorate
of all Indochina, and Japanese forces moved into the southern
half. At last, the United States acted. On 26 July 1941 all Japanese
assets in America were effectively frozen. Japan could not obtain

11

oil from America or the Dutch East Indies, nor any other strategic raw material. Japan's choice was now clear: either withdraw from her conquests and relinquish any plans for future conquests, or go to war. For the military caste in complete political control in Japan, the first choice would have been an unthinkable loss of face. So it was war. Furthermore, the date of war could be forecast. Japan had only the stocks of oil and other raw materials presently on hand. When they ran low, Japan would have to go to war to get more. It was like drawing a firm line across the bottom of a balance sheet, or setting light to the train of a fuse.

From 10 to 18 November the ships of Nagumo's striking force sailed from their several harbours in Japan and made their way, singly or in small groups, by various unobtrusive routes to their rendezvous at Tankan Bay, in Etorufu in the Kuriles. On the 20th, when all the force had assembled, Japan presented an ultimatum: her assets were to be restored, oil supplies resumed, and Japanese actions in China and Indochina virtually condoned. Understandably, these conditions were refused and the Americans presented their own ultimatum, equally unacceptable to the Japanese: Japan must withdraw from China and Indochina and recognize Chiang Kai-Shek's government. While the Japanese were refusing these demands, the last elements of their strike, an 'Advance Expeditionary Force' of sixteen submarines, five of them carrying two-man midget submarines to penetrate Pearl Harbor, had sailed from Kure.

On 27 November the U.S. Chief of Naval Operations Admiral Stark signalled to Kimmel in Pearl Harbor and Admiral Hart in Manila, ordering them to activate the defensive war plan known as 'Rainbow 5'. But the urgency of the order was greatly diminished by the addition of information suggesting that the Japanese were mounting an amphibious expedition against either the Philippines, the Thai or Kra peninsulas, or possibly Borneo. A Japanese fleet carrying five troop divisions had actually been reported off Formosa on 15 November, heading south. Japanese radio operators in Kure and elsewhere had kept up the volume of traffic to deceive American listeners after the fleet sailed and there was a considerable amount of diplomatic signal activity. But none of it pointed specifically to Pearl Harbor. In any case, nobody could believe that the Japanese could simultaneously launch attacks against the Philippines and Pearl Harbor. The big carriers would surely be needed to escort the southern invasion fleet (ironically, this was the very argument used by the over-ridden Nagano). Everbody underestimated the range and striking power of the latest Japanese naval aircraft. Nobody noted their recent feats in China. An attack on Pearl Harbor had been discussed as a real possibility earlier in the year but by the time it actually took place it had somehow dropped out of the collective staff consciousness; thus, in another Pearl Harbor paradox, the intelligence officers who studied Japanese intentions most closely

Japanese midget submarine
No. 19 beached after Pearl
Harbor

got the solution most wrong. A strike at Pearl Harbor demanded a kind of racial confidence, a naval arrogance in combat, which the Americans simply could not believe the Japanese possessed.

Admiral Kimmel and his staff were naturally affected by this prevailing climate of opinion. There were, too, difficulties in a divided command in Hawaii between the Navy and the Army, and even between departments of the Navy itself. Kimmel had to balance the requirement for flying long-distance search reconnaissance with the need to conserve the engine-hours of his few patrol aircraft. He also had to concentrate upon an energetic training programme, to prepare his fleet for a war which he knew must come—but not yet. Nevertheless, when all has been said, the U.S. Pacific Fleet had a 'five-day week' look about it. It could be counted upon to be in harbour every weekend and to be at ease, unbuckled, unprepared, on Sunday morning. Kimmel was after all in command of the most important American naval base in the Pacific, at a time when war was plainly imminent, and he should have been more watchful.

The Pearl Harbor Striking Force sailed from the bleak, snow-covered anchorage of Tankan Bay on the morning of 26 November. Admiral Nagumo flew his flag in the 26,900-ton *Akagi* ('Red Castle'), with the 26,000-ton *Kaga* ('Increased Joy'); these ships had been converted to carriers from a battle-cruiser and a battleship respectively. The new 20,000-ton carriers *Shokaku* ('Soaring Crane') and *Zuikaku* ('Happy Crane'), both completed in 1941, made up a second division; the smaller 10,500-ton carriers, *Hiryu* ('Flying Dragon') and *Soryu* ('Green Dragon'), both completed in the late 1930s, formed the third carrier division. The carriers had a close escort of a light cruiser and nine destroyers, and a supporting force, under Vice-Admiral Gunichi Mikawa, of two recently modernized 30-knot, 14-inch gunned *Kongo* Class battleships, *Hiei* and *Kirishima*, and two modern 8-inch gunned heavy cruisers, *Tone* and *Chikuma*. Two destroyers were allocated to bombard Midway, and the force was accompanied by a train of eight tankers and supply ships.

The striking force steered eastward into heavy seas, gales and thick fog which helped to conceal it. Secrecy was essential. Any British, Dutch or American ship met was to be sunk at sight, and any neutral boarded and prevented from sending radio signals. If the force was discovered, the attack was to be cancelled. The ship's companies were assembled and told of their objective, amid scenes of wild excitement and anticipation.

On 2 December Yamamoto broadcast the code message *Niitaka Yama Nobore* ('Climb Mount Niitaka'), authorizing the strike to go ahead, and confirmed the date 8 December Tokyo time, 7 December Hawaiian time. The weather moderated next day and the ships were able to refuel. On the evening of the 4th, when the force was about 900 miles north of Midway, course was altered to south-east. Early on the 6th Nagumo received the latest information on American ships in Pearl: seven battleships, seven cruisers, but no carriers. This was a severe disappointment, but Nagumo decided to go ahead. The battleships were still splendid prime targets, and the carriers might well return to harbour before the attack was launched. At 9 p.m. the striking force was still undetected, about 490 miles north of Oahu. The actual flag 'Z' flown by Togo's flagship *Mikasa* at Tsushima was hoisted to *Akagi's* masthead. In a state of high emotion, the force left the train behind and steered due south at 26 knots for the flying-off position, about 275 miles north of Pearl Harbor.

Meanwhile, at Pearl, there was already evidence that night that something unusual was happening. At 0542, the minesweeper *Condor* sighted the periscope of a midget submarine, which was sunk by the destroyer *Ward* after a search of two hours. Another midget entered through the anti-torpedo net which had been carelessly left open and was sunk by the destroyer *Monoghan*. A third midget ran aground after being attacked by the destroyer *Helm*. The last two of the five were probably sunk by destroyers during the night. Due to communications delays, unintelligent reporting and busy telephone lines, Admiral Kimmel did not hear of *Ward's* attack until shortly before 8 a.m. The first Japanese bombs were falling as he made his way to his office.

The Japanese navigation was excellent. In spite of the thick weather, which had prevented sun or star sights, Nagumo's force arrived at the launch point just before 6 a.m. and began to launch aircraft shortly afterwards. The strike flew in two parts: the first, led by Commander Mitsuo Fuchida, *Akagi's* air group commander, consisted of forty torpedo Kates, forty-nine Kates armed with 1,760-lb armour-piercing bombs, fifty-one Val dive-bombers and forty-three Zeke fighter escorts; the second, led by Lieutenant-Commander Shimazaki of *Zuikaku*, consisted of fifty-four Kates armed with 550-lb bombs, eighty Vals and another thirty-six Zekes for escort and ground-strafing, flew off an hour later.

Fuchida led his strike southwards through cloud and darkness until, just after 7 a.m., the sun rose on a brilliant day. As the

Banzai! Japanese carrier crew
cheering the Pearl Harbor
striking force

clouds rose, so did their hopes. At 7.40 they sighted the coastline, and nine minutes later Fuchida broadcast the attack message 'To . . .To . . .To . . .'

It was a beautifully peaceful morning, with church bells, calm water and bright early morning sunshine. Ashore, thoughts were on Sunday services, tennis, swimming, relaxation. On board, the watches were about to change and the ships were preparing for the ceremony of 'Colours', hoisting the ensign and jack. Above them, Fuchida was broadcasting 'TORA . . .TORA . . . TORA . . .' ('Tiger tiger, tiger')—'We have succeeded in a surprise attack.' 'Pearl Harbor was still asleep in the morning mist,' Commander Itaya, one of the pilots, recalled; 'it was calm and serene inside the harbour, not even a trace of smoke from the ships at Oahu. The orderly groups of barracks, the wriggling white line of the automobile road climbing up the mountain top, fine objectives of attack in all directions. In line with these, inside the harbour, were important ships of the Pacific Fleet, strung out and anchored two ships side by side in an orderly manner.'[2]

Fuchida's aircraft had been seen, flying down the west coast of Oahu, by civilians who thought they were air groups from *Lexington* and *Enterprise* returning, unusually early and on a Sunday, to Pearl Harbor. They were tracked by radar from Kahuku Point, the northernmost point of Oahu, by an army private under training who amused himself by plotting the

Banzai! Japanese carrier crew cheering the Pearl Harbor striking force

largest collection of radar echoes he had ever seen. His report was taken to refer to some B-17 Flying Fortresses expected on that bearing.

So the Japanese had a free hand. Not a gun was fired, not a plane rose in the air to meet them. Even when they attacked nobody believed it. Civilians seeing the smoke and hearing the noise thought it was a practice: 'That's good, we *ought* to get ready,' they said. Senior officers on the ground swore at the oncoming aircraft for breaking every local rule of air safety before noticing the red 'meatballs' on their wings. Ensign Joseph Taussig, in the battleship *Nevada*, looked across the water at the cruiser *Helena* and chuckled when he saw smoke pouring from her and imagined a chum of his on board her 'being reprimanded for blowing tubes while the wind was wrong. A split second later another thought flashed through my mind. *She was on fire*!'[3] At two minutes to eight, Rear-Admiral Bellinger broadcast the message which was received with incredulity in Washington and all over the world: AIR RAID PEARL HARBOR THIS IS NO DRILL.

While the alarm klaxons roared and the crews of every ship in Pearl Harbor went to General Quarters, many of the sailors still believing this was all a devilish drill designed to discomfort them on a Sunday morning, the torpedo-carrying Kates led by Lieutenant-Commander Shigehoru Murata attacked the ships alongside Ford Island from two sides, followed, high above, by

the bombing Kates, which were able to pick their targets at leisure. Some individuals, parties of men, and even whole ship's companies behaved with great resource and gallantry, reacting quickly to man their guns, counter-flood to counteract damage, provide power supplies and raise steam for sea. But in general the battle fleet was overwhelmed.

California, Admiral Pye's flagship, at the head of the line, was hit by two torpedoes deep under the water-line, and then by two bombs. The chaplain of the cruiser *New Orleans* watched a bomber attack *California* from across the harbour: 'I couldn't take my eyes off him. I followed him down until I saw the bombs drop out of his belly. Sticking out of the cockpit was the helmeted head of the Jap pilot. There was something mocking about the big rising-sun balls under the wings of the plane. The bombs hit her amidships, right by the stacks. A flash, fire and smoke jumped into the air all at once.'[4] The flagship, whose watertight integrity was impaired because compartment plates had been removed for a coming inspection, settled in the water until, three days later, only her superstructure was showing.

Astern of the flagship was *Oklahoma*, who was hit by three torpedoes and then by two more. She rolled over and capsized, until her masts stuck into the bottom mud. Inboard of her, *Maryland* was more fortunate, suffering only two bomb hits and the least casualties of any of the battleships. Astern of them again, *West Virginia* took six or seven torpedo and two bomb hits. She sank but quick counter-flooding prevented her from turning over. *Tennessee*, inboard of her, had two bomb hits, one of which killed her captain.

It was *Arizona*, astern of *Tennessee*, who suffered the worst fate. She was partly shielded by the repair ship *Vestal* alongside her but still had several bomb and torpedo hits. One heavy bomb (actually they were converted 16-inch shells) penetrated deep into the ship and detonated inside the forward magazine. The resulting explosion tore the forward half of the ship apart. *New Orlean*'s padre saw *Arizona* 'sending a mass of black, oily smoke thousands of feet into the air. The water round her was dotted with debris and a mass of bobbing oil-covered heads. I could see hundreds of men splashing and trying to swim. Others were motionless.'[5] Hundreds more never got out alive. A second bomb went down the funnel, and seven more hit the superstructure amidships. *Arizona* flooded and settled so fast that more than a thousand of her crew were trapped inside, burned or drowned.

Nevada, last in the line, was hit by one torpedo and two or three bombs but managed to shoot down two Kates and actually succeeded in raising steam and getting under way. As they passed the burning *Arizona* the men on the upperdeck had to keep wet cloths over their faces, the heat was so intense. As Taussig (whose men had shot down the Kates) said, 'We must have been within thirty yards of the burning ship and evidently we caught

Above: Towering smoke clouds from the crippled U.S. battleships *West Virginia* and *Tennessee*

Right: Pearl Harbor—American casualties were 3,435 killed or wounded while Japanese losses were under 100

fire from her, which augmented the flames from our own bomb hits.' On the other side of Ford Island, torpedo Kates sank the old battleship *Utah*, used as a target ship, and damaged the cruiser *Raleigh*.

While some of the Vals stayed to rake over the burning and listing battleships the majority under Lieutenant Commander Kakuichi Takahashi of *Shokaku* split into sections and attacked Ford Island, the U.S. Army air bases at Wheeler Field and at Hickam Field close to the harbour, the U.S. Navy seaplane base at Kaneohe Bay on the east coast, and the U.S. Marine Corps air base at Ewa, west of Pearl Harbor. There, they fell upon the rows of parked aircraft, placed neatly wingtip to wingtip, waiting like rows of chessmen to be toppled over. Zekes followed them down, knowing there was no opposition in the sky, to strafe buildings, vehicles, personnel and anything that moved.

At about 8.25 a.m. there was a lull of about a quarter of an hour, while the first wave withdrew. At 8.40 Shimazaki's Vals and Kates arrived overhead. They met much more anti-aircraft fire from the now thoroughly alerted ships and airfields and several Vals were shot down, but they still damaged the battleship *Pennsylvania* in dry dock and the destroyers *Cassin* and *Downes* ahead of her. One bomb blew off the bows of the destroyer *Shaw* in the floating dock. *Nevada* was attacked by Vals and forced to beach in shallow water to avoid blocking the main channel.

Suddenly, just before ten o'clock, the harbour went quiet. The aircraft disappeared. The roar of engines and the sound of bombs and guns were replaced by the crackling of the huge fires still burning, the shouts of first aid and damage control parties, and the cries of wounded men. At Pearl Harbor *Arizona*, *Oklahoma* and *Utah* had sunk and *West Virginia* and *California* were sinking. *Nevada* was beached and *Tennessee* badly on fire. The main battle fleet had been wiped out. *Pennsylvania*, *Helena*, *New Orleans*, *Honolulu*, *Curtiss*, *Raleigh*, *Shaw*, *Cassin* and *Downes* were all damaged. A total of 2,403 Navy, Army and Marine personnel and civilians had been killed and 1,178 wounded. Thirty-three naval aircraft had been destroyed at Ford Island, the same number at Ewa, eighteen at Hickam, all but two of the Catalinas at Kaneohe, and nearly all the aircraft at Wheeler Field. Of the 354 Japanese aircraft that took part, nine Zekes, fifteen Vals and five torpedo Kates were lost. They had left Pearl Harbor, and the United States as a whole, in a state of deep shock, after one of the worst defeats ever inflicted upon a nation in a single day.

Yet, in the end, it was not so bad. Fuchida and the other returning senior pilots tried to impress upon Nagumo the need for another strike. But Nagumo, who was not himself an aviator, had never shared Yamamoto's view of the attack on Pearl Harbor and cautiously decided that enough was enough. Japan had won a tremendous victory by any account. Another strike might overtax the kindliness of Japan's gods. He took his fleet away.

A civilian motorcar riddled by Japanese machine-gun fire eight miles from Pearl Harbor

This turned out to be a very serious error. The sunk battleships demonstrated their irrelevance in the war. The real weapon was to be the aircraft carrier with bomb- and torpedo-carrying aircraft. In any case, all but *Arizona* and *Oklahoma* eventually rejoined the fleet and were invaluable for bombardment. Had they been sunk in an action out at sea, they could not have been salvaged and would have been a total loss, along with perhaps 20,000 lives. As it was, the sunk and damaged battleships released large numbers of trained officers and men for other purposes, at a time when the U.S. Navy was expanding and personnel were in short supply.

The carriers escaped. *Lexington* was away, delivering a U.S. Marine bomber squadron to Midway Island. When the Japanese attacked, *Enterprise* was actually less than 200 miles west of Oahu, returning from delivering a U.S. Marine fighter squadron to Wake Island. *Saratoga*, the third U.S. Pacific Fleet carrier, was still on the West Coast of America. Even had the three been able to concentrate at sea, the Japanese, with a three-carrier advantage in numbers, a two-knot advantage in speed, and the inestimable morale advantage of recent success, might well have made short work of them.

The naval base also escaped. The massive docking and repair facilities built up over the previous ten years were almost untouched, as was the fuel depot, with some 4,500,000 barrels of fuel oil in storage. If those had been destroyed, the U.S. Pacific Fleet would have had to retreat to the West Coast and fight the early part of the war from there.

But the political effect of Pearl Harbor far outweighed the military and naval. Just after the last Japanese aircraft had left, Admiral Kimmel was handed a special war alert message from General Marshall in Washington, addressed to General Short in Hawaii. At about the time Nagumo had launched his strike that morning, a U.S. radio station had intercepted an important message to the Japanese Ambassador in Washington, ordering him to break of all diplomatic negotiations at 1300 Washington time. Stark received the message at 9.15 in Washington. It was pointed out that 1 p.m. in Washington was 7.30 a.m. in Hawaii. But some seventy minutes passed before General Marshall came back from his Sunday morning horse-ride and advised Stark to signal Kimmel. Stark demurred, thinking it was a false alarm. Marshall therefore telegraphed to Short and all army commanders, advising them to be on the alert. The message was too late, but this was the last diplomatic or communications dithering or hesitation. Pearl Harbor, at one blow, changed all that.

Pearl Harbor, at one blow, united the American nation behind the war effort as nothing else could have done. For over a year President Roosevelt had been publicly proclaiming that not one American boy would ever have to die overseas, whilst privily doing everything he could to further the Allied cause and to

change American pacifist thinking. Roosevelt had been having a hard time of it and had in fact only just persuaded Congress not to pass legislation reducing the armed forces even further. For the Japanese, Pearl Harbor had been subsidiary to their main intent in South-east Asia. It had been intended only to cripple the U.S. fleet in order to gain time whilst Japan consolidated her conquests and then, when the British and Americans were weary of a two-ocean war, obtain peace terms favourable to Japan. There had been no need to attack American possessions; indeed, it had been Roosevelt's great fear that Japan would move from conquest to conquest in the east whilst America remained helpless and bound by treaty. At one blow Pearl Harbor changed all that, and in that sense it came as a political relief.

Mixed with the American fury at the treacherous nature of the attack, the grief over the lives lost, and the determination to gain revenge, was a curious element of outrage, only to be explained by the special American relationship with the Japanese. It was America that had introduced Japan to the West and to Western methods. Many Japanese lived in the States. Americans tended to think of the Japanese as an amiable, polite, toothily grinning, harmless race who made good manservants. Pearl Harbor was therefore like being leaped on and savaged by a favourite lapdog.

Nobody understood the effect of Pearl Harbor upon the American nation and on long-term strategy better than Winston Churchill. He did not conceal his jubilation. 'So we had won after all!' he wrote. 'We had won the war. England would live; Britain would live; the Commonwealth of Nations and the Empire would live. How long the war would last or in what fashion it would end no man could tell, nor did I at this moment care. Once again in our long island history we should emerge, however mauled and mutilated, safe and victorious. We should not be wiped out. Our history would not come to an end. We might not even have to die as individuals. Hitler's fate was sealed. Mussolini's fate was sealed. As for the Japanese, they would be ground to a powder.' Once again, Churchill produced the perfect metaphor. 'I thought of a remark which Edward Grey had made to me more than thirty years before—that the United States is like "a gigantic boiler. Once the fire is lighted under it there is no limit to the power it can generate." Being saturated and satiated with emotion and sensation, I went to bed and slept the sleep of the saved and thankful.'[6]

Not many people that night could have gone to bed thinking of Pearl Harbor as salvation, but proof that Churchill was right soon came in an ominous, vengeful voice from Pearl Harbor itself, making the first of many quotable quotes. When Vice-Admiral William F. Halsey Jr, who had been flying his flag in *Enterprise*, came back and saw what had been done to Pearl Harbor, he vowed, 'Before we're through with them, the Japanese language will be spoken only in hell!'[7]

Opposite: The U.S. destroyers *Downes* (left) and *Cassin* (foreground) badly damaged in dry dock and (background) the battleship *Pennsylvania*, also damaged

2 RETREAT IN THE EAST

As the aircraft carrying Admiral Chester W. Nimitz flew over Pearl Harbor on Christmas morning, 1941, the new C.-in-C. Pacific looked down at the harbour, whose waters were still stained black with spilled fuel oil. *Oklahoma* and *Utah* were lying bottom up at their berths. All that could be seen of *California*, *Arizona* and *West Virginia* were their blackened and blasted super-structures sticking out of the water. When Nimitz climbed into a motorboat to go ashore, he could smell the oil, the charred wood and blistered paint, and the foul odour of decaying flesh from the bodies which still surfaced every day in the harbour and the hundreds more trapped in the *Arizona*.

The news matched the view. Simultaneously with the attack on Pearl Harbor, General Yamashita's XXV Army landed at Singora and Patani, on the Kra Isthmus of Thailand and at Kota Bharu in Malaya, quickly captured the local airfields, and began to advance southwards, driving increasingly exhausted and demoralized British and Indian forces before them. The battleship *Prince of Wales* and the battle-cruiser *Repulse* were sent from Singapore to disrupt the Japanese landings. Instead, they were themselves attacked in the South China Sea, east of Malaya, on the afternoon of 10 December by Japanese bombers and torpedo-bombers flying from bases near Saigon. The Japanese struck at a range and with a concerted skill nobody previously had believed them capable of, and both ships, lacking fighter cover, sank to repeated bomb and torpedo hits, with the loss of 840 men, including Admiral Sir Tom Phillips, the force commander. This double blow was felt more deeply in Britain than any other the country had suffered at sea. Schoolboys at home in England went down to breakfast that morning and knew by their parents' faces that something terrible had happened. Churchill himself said that on hearing the news he never in all the war received a more direct shock. It was a severe strategic setback for the Allies, a shocking tactical defeat for the Royal Navy, and a great personal tragedy for the officers and men involved. It was also to be the first time for hundreds of years that the Royal Navy lost its supremacy in any theatre of war at sea and failed eventually to regain it. The U.S. Navy assumed the mantle in the Far East on that day and when the Royal Navy reappeared in strength it was still as a junior partner.

In the Philippines, General Homma's XIV Army began with a landing on Batan Island, in the north of the archipelago, on 10 December and followed with a landing on south Luzon on the 12th and a major landing at Lingayen Gulf on the 20th, having by then smashed the U.S. Far East Army Air Force. By 23 December Yamashita's men in Malaya had reached the Perak River. On Christmas Eve Homma's army landed at Lamon Bay. General MacArthur's original plan to defeat the Japanese on the beaches had patently failed and he decided upon a retreat to the Bataan Peninsula and a fight to the last ditch. Also on Christmas

Eve Wake Island surrendered, after a prolonged and gallant defence by the U.S. Marine garrison, but in circumstances which did no credit to the U.S. Navy Pacific Command. On Christmas Day itself Hong Kong surrendered. Guam had already fallen, on 10 December. Everywhere in the Far East, Japanese forces were going forward like a tide at the flood, reaching far up into every harbour and inlet, circling high points of resistance, but flowing ever onwards as though nothing could ever stop them.

Nimitz spent no time in fruitless moping. Briskly, he told the staff officers at Pearl that he had perfect confidence in them and that those who wished to serve on his staff could do so. There was to be no witch-hunt. Morale began to rise. Nimitz read himself in as CincPac on the deck of the submarine *Grayling* on 31 December. He chose her because he was himself a submariner and, as he used to say somewhat sardonically, because the Japanese had left him no other sort of deck at Pearl.

The best thumbnail sketch of Nimitz is still that by the American historian S. E. Morison.

'Chester Nimitz was one of those rare men who grow as their responsibilities increase; but even at the end of the war, when his staff had expanded to 636 officers and he had almost 5,000 ships and over 16,000 planes under his command, he retained the simplicity of his Texas upbringing. Ever calm and gentle in demeanor and courteous in speech, he had tow-coloured hair turning white, blue eyes and a pink complexion which gave him somewhat the look of a friendly small boy, so that war correspondents, who expected admirals to pound the table and bellow as in the movies, were apt in wonder 'Is this the man?' He was the man. No more fortunate appointment to this vital command could have been made. He restored confidence to the defeated Fleet. He had the patience to wait through the lean period of the war, the capacity to organise both a fleet and a vast theater, the tact to deal with sister services and Allied commands, the leadership to weld his own subordinates into a great fighting team, the courage to take necessary risks, and the wisdom to select, from a welter of intelligence and opinion, the strategy that defeated Japan.'[8]

On 20 December, Admiral Ernest J. King, formerly the C.-in-C. Atlantic Fleet, was appointed C.-in-C. U.S. Fleet (COMINCH). 'Ernie' King was an austere, unforgiving character and a notable Anglophobe, who was supposed in the popular mythology of the U.S. Navy to shave with a blow-torch. On Christmas Eve he issued his first statement:

The way to victory is long
The going will be hard.
We will do the best we can with what we've got.
We must have more planes and ships—at once.
Then it will be our turn to strike.
We will win through—in time.

Bataan, 1942. Japanese troops celebrate the capture of an American gun

It took a big man to make such a pronouncement on the very day of the surrender of Wake Island (which was not announced to the public or to the rest of the Navy). Wake had first been attacked on 8 December and a Japanese invasion force arrived there on the 11th. The Marine garrison, never more than some 500 strong, put up a tremendous resistance, shooting down twenty-one Japanese aircraft in all and sinking two Japanese destroyers, *Kayate* and *Kisaragi*, the first Japanese warships to be sunk in surface action in the war. But Wake's resources had always been thin and when another invasion force arrived on the 22nd, the last defending fighter was shot down and the garrison's situation became desperate. Help was actually on the way: the carrier *Saratoga*, three 8-inch gun cruisers and nine destroyers, with an oiler, under Rear-Admiral Frank Jack Fletcher. On 22 December this force was only 515 miles from Wake but spent the next day fuelling, steaming north instead of west, and ended the day further from

Japanese Marines watching
their artillery shell a U.S.
strongpoint in the Philippines

Guam, 1941. Three men about
to be executed by the Japanese
kneel before their own graves

below: Japanese light tanks in a victory parade in the Philippines

Wake than at the beginning. In the *interregnum* period between Kimmel's relief and Nimitz's assuming command, the U.S. fleet was commanded by Admiral Pye, a very cautious officer. Pye decided there was no hope of relieving Wake and ordered Fletcher to turn back—an order which caused consternation in *Saratoga*, whose aircrews were almost mutinous with frustration. (On Wake the Marine prisoners of war hoped against hope that they would be rescued until they were taken away from the island on 12 January.) The news was received with great bitterness at Pearl Harbor, where the Navy's morale sank even lower. It was the blackest Christmas anybody could ever remember.

Nor did the New Year of 1942 bring much cheer. The Japanese conquest seemed to gain momentum as it went on. The Japanese moved forward in a rapid succession of amphibious operations, each one an advance of about 400 miles, but never further than shore or carrier aircraft could give cover: Sarawak on 23 December, Brunei on 6 January, Tarakan on the 10th, Jesselton on the 11th, Balikpapan on the 24th, Kendari in the Celebes on the 24th, Makasar on 9 February, Timor on the 20th, always moving closer to the final objective, Java. The priceless strategic position of Rabaul was taken on 23 January. In the Philippines, Homma's army had broken through decisively at Cabanatuan on 29 December. In Malaya Yamashita had won a decisive battle at the Slim River on 7 January and entered Kuala Lumpur on the 11th. On the 20th the Japanese began a major offensive northwards into Burma, and within weeks had inflicted major defeats, amounting to disasters, upon British and Indian troops at the Binin and Sittang rivers.

Here and there, isolated naval actions attempted to stem the tide. By 17 January the Japanese had completed their easy capture of Tarakan in Borneo and were ready for their next objective of Balikpapan. Sixteen troop transports with three escorting patrol vessels sailed on the 21st, and were soon sighted by submarines and by Catalinas. A covering force of a cruiser and nine destroyers and other light craft, under Admiral Nishimura, steamed eastward to prevent any interference by Allied ships after the transports had arrived. A striking force under Vice-Admiral W. A. Glassford U.S.N. had already sailed from Timor but the cruiser *Boise* hit an uncharted submarine pinnacle and another cruiser *Marblehead* could only make 15 knots, on one engine, so the old four-funnelled destroyers, *John D. Ford*, *Pope*, *Parrott* and *Paul Jones* went on by themselves, under Commander Talbot in *John D. Ford*, arriving off the Japanese troop anchorage in the early hours of the 24 January.

It was a destroyer man's dream: a night torpedo and gun attack against unsuspecting targets, at anchor. The destroyers weaved in and out of the lines of troopships at high speed, firing torpedoes at targets as they appeared and, judging by the satisfying sounds of explosions, doing great execution. Nishimura suspected a submarine attack and won the 'leather medal' by somewhat unintelligently leading his ships out to sea, away from his enemy. In exchange for one hit on *Ford*, doing some damage, the destroyers claimed the destruction of the entire troop convoy. The cold light of dawn and post-war research showed that the tally was rather less: four transports out of a possible twelve, one patrol vessel out of three. However, it was the U.S. Navy's first surface engagement of the war, in fact their first since Santiago de Cuba during the Spanish-American War in July 1898, and it was certainly successful. It was good for morale. But, as the Japanese said, it did not delay their invasion by a single day.

The Japanese had allowed a hundred days for the conquest of Malaya and their programme ran well ahead of schedule. The last British and Indian troops crossed the causeway from Johore to Singapore Island on 31 January. The Japanese began their assault on the island on 8 February. General Percival, the army commander, surrendered Singapore on Sunday the 15th, after seventy days of the least competent campaigns ever fought by any British general.

But the black political gloom and miserably incompetent military leadership were redeemed by acts of startling individual bravery. On 13 February, the ex-Yangtse river steamer *Li Wo*, commissioned by the Royal Navy as an auxiliary patrol vessel, sailed from Singapore for Java. She had a scratch crew, including survivors from other ships, and many passengers. Her captain was an ex-Merchant Navy officer Lieutenant 'Tam' Wilkinson R.N.R., an old 'China hand' who had knocked about the Far East in various ships for twenty years before the war. On the 14th, off the Sumatran coast, several Japanese ships were sighted, escorted by a cruiser and other warships. *Li Wo* was armed only with one ancient 4-inch gun and two machine guns, but Wilkinson unhesitatingly attacked. He had never had a lecture on tactics in his life but by brilliant ship-handling stayed in action against the cruiser for over an hour. *Li Wo* was inevitably hit and badly damaged and Wilkinson himself ended the action by ramming a Japanese transport previously hit and set on fire by *Li Wo's* venerable gun. *Li Wo* sank, with only ten survivors. Wilkinson was not one of them. In 1946, when the true facts came to light, he was awarded a posthumous Victoria Cross.

The ships Wilkinson had attacked were part of a Japanese invasion convoy bound for Sumatra. Japanese airborne troops had dropped on the important oil refineries at Palembang on 14 February and the main invasion force landed the next day. On the 19th the Japanese landed at Bali, thus isolating Java from the east and west, and the same day launched a heavy, punishing air strike against Port Darwin in northern Australia. This raid was the first time carrier and shore-based aircraft co-operated in a major strike. Admiral Nagumo, with a strong force of four carriers, two battleships and three cruisers, had entered the Banda

Sea undetected and unmolested. In two raids, the first of 188 carrier planes and the second of 54 from Kendari in the Celebes, the Japanese brushed aside the slight fighter and anti-aircraft defences of Darwin and sank the U.S. destroyer *Peary*, four American transports, a British tanker and four other Australian ships, as well as destroying ten aircraft. Some 240 people were killed and another 150 wounded. Shore installations and harbour works were bombed and strafed and Darwin was put out of action as a base for several months. The Darwin strike, with another at Broome further along the coast on 4 March, when sixteen flying boats and seven other aircraft were destroyed, were defensive measures, designed to prevent Allied interference with the Japanese invasion of Java. But this was the first time the war had come home to Australian soil. Many Australians understandably thought the raids were preludes to an invasion, and they therefore caused alarm and despondency out of all proportion to the physical damage they achieved.

At that time, when the Japanese were running everything before them, the Allied defence of the East had largely to be improvised, and perhaps the greatest improvisation of all was the creation of the ABDA (American-British-Dutch-Australian) Command early in January, with Field-Marshall Wavell as Supreme Commander. (Wavell said, when he heard of his appointment, 'I've heard of holding the baby, but this is twins!') ABDA was supposed to conduct the defence of Burma, Malaya, the Dutch East Indies, the Philippines, the Christmas and Cocos islands, the Andamans and the Nicobars. But it had been formed far too late and its task was hopeless. ABDA was dissolved on 25 February after Wavell's unanswerable comment that there was nothing left to command.

By that time the only effective force left to ABDA was the Combined Striking Force of American, Dutch, British and Australian ships under Admiral Helfrich, who relieved Admiral Hart U.S.N. on 25 February. The ships did their best, but bad luck, lack of air support, and the Japanese Navy took a steady toll of them. On 4 February the Dutch Admiral Karel Doorman had led the Dutch cruiser *De Ruyter*, flying his flag, the American cruisers *Houston* and *Marblehead*, the small Dutch cruiser *Tromp*, four Dutch and three American destroyers to attack a Japanese invasion convoy assembling at Balikpapan. Their route was long and exposed to air attack and, lacking air cover, the ships were duly attacked. *De Ruyter*, *Houston* and *Marblehead* were all damaged—*Marblehead* so badly she had to go back to America for repairs.

On 18 February Doorman, an unlucky admiral, led another sortie against the Japanese invasion convoy heading for Bali. The Dutch destroyer *Kortenaer* grounded and had to be left behind. In a night battle in the Lombok Strait, the Dutch destroyer *Piet Hein* was sunk and *Tromp* so badly damaged she

Bataan, Philippine Islands—
the face of defeat

had to be sent to Australia for repairs. One Japanese destroyer and a transport were damaged.

The Japanese were now ready to invade Java. A Western Invasion Force sailed in fifty-six transports from Cam Ranh Bay in Indochina. The Eastern Invasion Force, of forty-one transports, escorted by two heavy and two light cruisers and 14 destroyers, was sighted on 27 February. Once more, Doorman led his ships to sea. With five cruisers—*De Ruyter*, the Dutch *Java*, *Houston*, whose after turret was still out of action from the 18th, the Australian *Perth* and the British *Exeter*—and nine destroyers, Doorman was only slightly numerically inferior to the Japanese. But the Japanese made deadly use of a weapon the Allies had never suspected: the 60.9-cm, Type 93 oxygen-powered 'Long Lance' torpedo, which had the phenomenal running range of 44,000 yards at 36 knots. In a battle in the Java Sea, the Japanese sank *De Ruyter* and *Java*, the British destroyers *Electra* and *Jupiter* and the Dutch *Kortenaer*. Admiral Doorman went down in *De Ruyter*. The same day, the American aircraft tender *Langley* was badly damaged by shore-based bombers and had to be scuttled.

Houston and *Perth* reached Batavia on the 28th, refuelled and sailed that evening for Tjilatjap. They encountered part of a Japanese convoy at Bantam Bay, east of the Sunda Strait, and destroyed four transports but were then themselves sunk by the Japanese covering force of three cruisers and nine destroyers. The Dutch destroyer *Evertsen* was so badly damaged she had to be beached. The next day, 1 March, *Exeter*, which had been badly damaged on the 27th, and the destroyers *Encounter* and *Pope* sailed from Surabaya, and were also sunk.

The Allied ships had been led by a fatally unlucky admiral, had been bedevilled by communications difficulties, had had little opportunity to exercise together, lacked air cover, and were faced by an enemy who possessed the devastating Long Lance and ample strike and reconnaissance aircraft. Their forlorn battles, as Churchill called them, delayed the Japanese invasion by only twenty-four hours. The Japanese came ashore in western and eastern Java during the night of 28 February/1 March. The Dutch East Indies Government in Java surrendered unconditionally on 8 March. In Burma, Rangoon fell on the 9th. In the Philippines, the surviving American and Filipino forces had been driven into the Bataan Peninsula, and on the 12th General MacArthur left for Australia, on the orders of President Roosevelt, though vowing he would return.

The Japanese carriers could have struck again at Hawaii, or even at the American West Coast, which was still only sketchily defended in the air. Instead, they chose to strike westwards, into the Indian Ocean. On 28 March Allied intelligence reported a powerful Japanese raiding force heading west. The surviving ships of the British Eastern Fleet had retreated to Colombo, where Admiral Sir James Somerville, one of the Navy's most successful

wartime officers, arrived to take over as C.-in-C. Sir James was a bold, witty and outspoken man, with the common touch and a somewhat Rabelaisian sense of humour. On first seeing his fleet at sea he signalled to them: 'So this is the Eastern Fleet. Well never mind. There's many a good tune played on an old fiddle.'[9] The fleet, containing every ship a hard-pressed Admiralty could muster, looked impressive enough on paper: five battleships, three aircraft carriers, seven cruisers and fourteen destroyers. But four of the battleships, *Resolution*, *Ramillies*, *Royal Sovereign* and *Revenge*, were very old, very slow and of very short endurance. One of the carriers, *Hermes*, was also old, slow and small and the air groups of the other two, *Formidable* and *Indomitable*, lacked battle practice. Nevertheless, whatever its shortcomings the Eastern Fleet was still 'a fleet in being' and as such a threat to the flank of the Japanese invasion in Burma.

Somerville, flying his flag in *Warspite*, assembled his ships at sea on 31 March in two tactical units: a fast Force A under his own command, and a slow Force B under his second in command, Vice-Admiral Algernon Willis. Lacking recent information on the strength or position of the Japanese, Somerville hoped to engage them by night with a torpedo attack by Albacores from *Indomitable*, while Force B stayed in support.

In the event, shortage of fuel forced Somerville's ships back to the fleet base at Addu Atoll, in the Maldive Islands, before the Japanese could be brought to action. Characteristically, Somerville was very disappointed at what he thought was a lost chance. 'I fear', he wrote, 'they have taken fright, which is a pity because if I could have given them a good crack now it would have been timely.'[10]

It might have been timely, but it would have been very unlikely. With hindsight, it can now be seen that Somerville was very lucky indeed not to meet the Japanese, for the raiders were actually Nagumo's formidable Striking Force, with five of the six carriers which had attacked Pearl Harbor, four fast battleships, two cruisers and some destroyers. Barring a miracle, a fleet engagement would have been yet another shattering disaster to the Fleet.

Above left: The cruiser *Cornwall* sinking after Japanese air attack, 5 April 1942

Centre: *Cornwall* and *Dorsetshire* manoeuvring violently under dive-bombing attack, 5 April 1942

Right: The carrier *Hermes* sinking after ten bomb hits in forty minutes, 9 April 1942

Thwarted in his efforts to find the Eastern Fleet, Nagumo made short work of whatever targets he could find. While Vice-Admiral Ozawa, with one carrier, cruisers and destroyers raided the east coast of India, Nagumo's aircraft fell upon Colombo harbour on Easter Sunday, 5 April. But the harbour had been cleared beforehand, and although some twenty aircraft were shot down Colombo was not put out of action as Darwin had been. On the same day Japanese dive-bombers found and sank the cruisers *Cornwall* and *Dorsetshire*, who had been on their way to rejoin the fleet. Many of their people were lost in the action and many more to shark attack while waiting to be picked up. On 9 April, off the east coast of Ceylon, *Hermes*, the destroyer *Vampire*, the corvette *Hollyhock* and two tankers were also bombed and sunk. While the Japanese raiders retired triumphantly eastward, Somerville's slow Force B withdrew to Mombasa, while Force A went to Bombay. From now on, Admiral Somerville would, in his own words, 'have to lie low in one sense but be pretty active in another; keep the old tarts out of the picture and roar about with the others'.[11]

On the day *Hermes* was sunk, the Americans and Filipinos on Bataan surrendered. The survivors were subjected to a sixty-five mile 'Death March' on which they were denied food and water and compelled to march under a tropical sun for long periods without rest, being clubbed and bayoneted as they went along. On 6 May Corregidor, the last Allied stronghold in the Philippines, surrendered. In the north, the British and Indian troops of the Eastern Army in Burma were approaching the Assam frontier, after a retreat of 1,000 miles—the longest in British military history. In six months, the Japanese had established their Greater Asia Co-Prosperity Sphere, an empire of 90,000,000 people stretching from Rabaul to Rangoon and containing 88 per cent of the world's rubber, 54 per cent of its tin, 30 per cent of its rice, 20 per cent of its tungsten, and the rich oilfields of the East Indies. All this they had done at the cost of some 15,000 men, about 400 aircraft and a couple of dozen warships, none of them larger than a destroyer.

3 CORAL SEA: THE TURNING POINT

It was at this point, when the Far Eastern world rang with their victories, when they really did seem invincible, at sea, in the air and in the jungle, that the Japanese overreached themselves. Nagumo's aircrews returned to Japan on 18 April like the conquering heroes they were, most of them suffering from what the Japanese themselves called 'Victory Disease', a very human affliction which the Greeks knew as *hubris*. For the Greeks it was almost always followed by *nemesis*. The Americans had just as expressive a term: Japan was very shortly to receive her 'come-uppance'.

The American carriers had escaped at Pearl Harbor, and this omission was like a thread left untied which ultimately allowed the whole fabric of Japanese conquest to be unravelled. Yamamoto himself had promised that he would run free for the first six months of the war. After that, he was not so sure. King had ordered Nimitz to hold 'at all costs' a line running from Midway south to Samoa, Fiji and Brisbane. The carrier *Saratoga* was torpedoed by a Japanese submarine and badly damaged on 11 January, some 500 miles south-east of Oahu, but she was replaced by *Yorktown*. In the early months of 1942 the three carriers *Yorktown*, *Lexington* and *Enterprise* crossed Nimitz's defensive line and began cautiously to carry the war back to the Japanese.

On 1 February 1942 Task Force 17, headed by Halsey in *Enterprise*, attacked the northern Marshall Islands, while TF 8, led by Fletcher in *Yorktown*, struck at the islands in the south. Halsey had a hectic day of air strikes, surface bombardments, air alarms and Japanese bombing attacks, including one semi-suicide attack by a large Japanese bomber on *Enterprise*. As Robert J. Casey of the *Chicago Daily News* said, it was 'everything you could ask for except a cavalry charge'.[12] After nine hours of furious activity Halsey retired, leaving several Japanese ships sunk at Kwajalein Atoll. Further south Fletcher had less success, but nevertheless this was something like good news for America at last, and the press made much of it. 'Bull' Halsey became America's first naval hero of the war and from then on he never left the war correspondents short of material.

On 21 February Admiral Wilson Brown led a force including *Lexington* in an even bolder sortie against Rabaul. They were sighted and attacked but the heavy force of Japanese bombers was engaged and repulsed in a frantic series of dog-fights which took place above the fleet, to the cheers of the spectators. Wilson Brown said: 'I even had to remind some members of my staff that this was not a football game.' Five Kates were shot down (one tried to hit *Lexington* in its fall). Morale in the American carriers soared. 'Lady Lex' became the best known ship in the Pacific.

After raids by *Enterprise*'s aircraft on Wake Island on 24 February and Marcus Island on 4 March, *Lexington* and *Yorktown* combined for the most daring venture yet, through the Coral Sea and into the Gulf of Papua, only some forty-five miles off the

Opposite: Coral Sea, 1942. The crew of the carrier *Lexington* abandoning ship

southern shores of the island. On 10 March, 100 carrier planes crossed the 7,500-foot Owen Stanley range of mountains and attacked shipping at Lae and Salamaua. They sank a large minesweeper, a 6,000-ton transport and a light cruiser.

These raids were excellent for American morale but, in fact, as one officer said 'the Japs didn't mind them any more than a dog minds a flea'. In April, however, a raid took place which the Japanese minded very much. On the 18th, about 700 miles east of Japan, sixteen B-25 Mitchell bombers of the U.S. Army led by General James Doolittle took off from *Hornet*. The B-25s were so big that they prevented *Hornet* operating her own aircraft while they were on board, and she had been escorted to the launch point by Halsey in *Enterprise*. The force was sighted early on the 18th and surprise was lost so it was decided to launch the strike at once. (This baffled the Japanese, who calculated that a strike by normal carrier-borne aircraft could not be launched until the following morning.) 'The wind and sea were so strong that morning', Halsey wrote years later, 'that green water was breaking over the carriers' ramps. Jimmy led his squadron off. When his plane buzzed down the *Hornet*'s deck at 0725, there wasn't a man topside in the Task Force who didn't help sweat him into the air. One pilot hung on the brink of a stall until we nearly catalogued his effects, but the last of the sixteen was airborne by 0824, and a minute later my staff officer was writing in the flag log, "Changed fleet course and axis to 90°, commencing retirement from the area at 25 knots." '13

Thirteen B-25s bombed Tokyo and the other three dropped incendiaries on Nagoya, Osaka and Kobe. The aircraft then flew on and landed where they could, one of them in the sea off Ningpo, and four crash-landed. Of the eighty aircrew on the raid, seventy-one survived: one was killed in his parachute descent, four were drowned, three were executed by the Japanese and one died in prison. 'Doolittle's Raid', as it was called, was an enormous publicity success for the United States and baffled and alarmed the Japanese, who, like the citizens of Berlin, had believed they were immune from air attack. These sixteen aircraft which, for all the Japanese knew, might have taken off from 'Shangri La', as Roosevelt sardonically said, had an effect on the progress of the war out of all proportion to the minor amount of physical damage they actually did. They served to concentrate sharply the Japanese debate on future strategy.

The Japanese had achieved their war objectives, especially the supply of oil, so quickly and completely that the Imperial General Staff had given little thought to the future. Japan now had a choice of offensive strategies. She could strike west, with invasions of Ceylon and southern India, aiming for an eventual link with the forces of the Wehrmacht in the Middle East; or she could move south and invade Australia. Both these alternatives were favoured by the Naval General Staff, but not by the Army,

'There wasn't a man topside in the Task Force who didn't help sweat him into the air.' An army B-25 Mitchell bomber takes off from the carrier *Hornet* on Doolittle's Raid

whose thoughts were on China and particularly on a possible offensive against the old enemy, Russia. A third choice was to strike east, at Midway and Hawaii, and in the process provoke a major fleet action in which the main U.S. Pacific Fleet with its carriers would be utterly and finally destroyed, leading to the possibility then of a negotiated peace. The destruction of the American fleet was a consummation very dear to the hearts of Yamamoto, C.-in-C. Combined Fleet, and his staff. The Naval General Staff preferred a modified plan; if not an actual invasion of Australia, then at least a drive to isolate her from her Allies by seizing the chains of islands running south-east from the tip of New Guinea through the Solomons, the New Hebrides and the Fijis to Samoa. They had already begun to put this plan into effect with landings at Lae and Salamaua in New Guinea in March 1942.

Yamamoto himself was always conscious that time was running against Japan. The sooner the U.S. fleet was 'taken out' the better. The longer they waited the stronger the Americans would be. The Doolittle Raid served to strengthen Yamamoto's argument for an attack on Midway. The cheek of it, the sheer unbelievable audacity of a bombing attack on sacred Japanese soil and the unthinkable possibility of a menace to the Emperor's sacred person,

made it all the more imperative that the American fleet be destroyed. The capture of Midway would give the Japanese a vital strategic outpost, and would inevitably bring on a conflict with the American Pacific Fleet. Nimitz could not stand by and watch Midway invaded.

In the event, the Japanese Naval General Staff compromised: they agreed to continue with the advance towards the Solomons, *and* the attack on Midway. The first part of the plan was to begin in May with landings at Tulagi in the Solomons and at Port Moresby on the south-eastern tip of Papua. The second part, the landing on Midway, was to follow in June. The way to the crucial battles of the Coral Sea and Midway was now open. So, also, was the path to Japan's defeat, for as the American war effort gathered momentum and strength Japan would have been hard-pressed to keep what she had already won. These two new offensives, with the continuing campaigns in China and Burma, were more than she could sustain.

For the Allies, Churchill and Roosevelt had agreed at the Arcadia Conference in Washington in January 1942 that the first priority should be the war against Germany. Strategy in the Pacific must for the moment remain on the defensive, containing the Japanese wherever possible, until a turn for the better in the European war and the growing military power of the United States enabled the Allies to take the offensive. After ABDA's unlamented demise, Great Britain kept strategic responsibility for the Indian Ocean, Malaya and Sumatra, while the United States assumed responsibility for the whole of the Pacific, including Australia and New Zealand. MacArthur was appointed Supreme Allied Commander, South-west Pacific, while Nimitz became C.-in-C. Pacific Ocean Area.

The Japanese could have assembled an invasion force, given it the strongest available escort, and simply sent it to occupy Port Moresby. But that was not their way. Whenever possible, the Japanese liked to over-elaborate, splitting their forces into separate groups with separate objectives, inviting defeat in detail. They laid intricate traps, with complicated diversions, sacrificial decoys and optimistic pincer movements. Japanese plans demanded a degree of co-operation between their own ships and commanders which no navy in history has ever achieved. They made few allowances for the contingencies of war. Most dangerous of all, they often relied upon the enemy doing what was expected of him.

Task Force MO, for the capture of Port Moresby, was a typically complicated Japanese undertaking. An invasion group of six destroyers, eleven transports and miscellaneous minesweepers and oilers, under Rear-Admiral Sadamichi Kajioka in the cruiser *Yubari*, was to sail from Rabaul on 4 May. A smaller group of minelayers, transports and two destroyers was to invade Tulagi in the Solomons and set up a seaplane base there. A support group

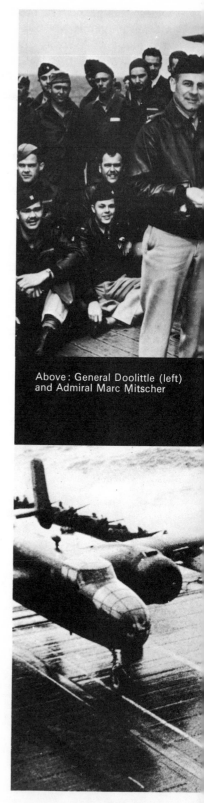

Above: General Doolittle (left) and Admiral Marc Mitscher

40

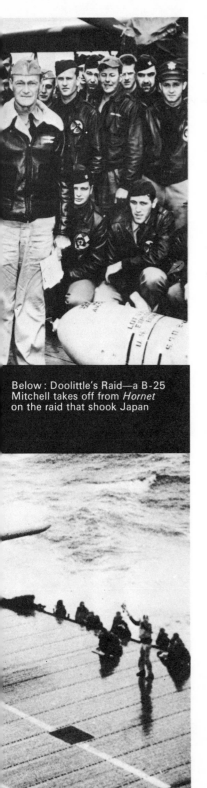

Below: Doolittle's Raid—a B-25 Mitchell takes off from *Hornet* on the raid that shook Japan

including the seaplane carrier *Kamikawa Maru* was to establish a similar base in the Louisiades Islands. The main covering group, under Rear-Admiral Aritomo Goto, with four heavy cruisers and the light carrier *Shoho*, was to support first the Tulagi and then the Port Moresby landing. A striking force of two heavy cruisers, *Zuikaku* and *Shokaku*, under Vice-Admiral Takeo Takagi was to sail from Truk, round the eastern end of the Solomons and enter the Coral Sea from the east. The whole operation was commanded by the C.-in-C. Fourth Fleet, Vice-Admiral Shigeyoshi Inouye, at Rabaul, who also had the (not always easily biddable) support of the land-based 25th Air Flotilla. The intention was that any Allied force attempting to molest the Port Moresby landing would be caught between the pincers of Goto's force to the west and Takagi's carriers to the east. Once this Allied force had been destroyed, Japan would control the Coral Sea and be able to neutralize air bases in Queensland before going on to invade the Ocean and Nauru islands, whose phosphates would be valuable for Japanese agriculture. It was an ambitious, ingenious, and indeed feasible plan; but for tricks of weather and inexplicable errors by the Japanese air groups, it might have worked.

At Pearl Harbor, Nimitz and his staff had the priceless advantage of knowing the Japanese intentions. The cracking of the top-secret Japanese 'purple' naval code, the constant surveillance and imaginative interpretation of all Japanese radio traffic, and the invaluable assistance of 'coast-watchers', most of them Australians, left behind on Japanese-occupied islands together gave Nimitz an extraordinarily accurate forecast of Japanese planning. Warning was received of an impending operation as early as 16 April. It was probably planned to start on 3 May, and intelligence appreciation suggested Port Moresby as the likeliest target.

Port Moresby was vital, and had to be defended. It was not only the key-point for the protection of Australia, but an essential launching stage for future Allied offensives. However, it was one thing to know the Japanese intentions, but quite another to defeat them. There were some 300 U.S.A.A.F. and R.A.A.F. aircraft based in Australia available for long-range search and attack missions, but their aircrews were inexperienced in identifying and attacking shipping (as the coming battle would demonstrate) and in any case the aircraft were in General MacArthur's South-west Pacific Command. The Combined Chiefs of Staff had already approved strict rules of demarcation between the two commands. Nimitz would just have to hope for what co-operation he could get from MacArthur.

Clearly, the main effort would have to come from Nimitz's own carriers. He sent Task Force 11, with *Lexington*, under Rear-Admiral Aubrey W. Fitch, south to rendezvous with Task Force 17, commanded by Fletcher in *Yorktown*, in the Coral Sea approaches west of the New Hebrides on 1 May. Another force of two Australian heavy cruisers, *Australia* and *Hobart*, the U.S.

cruiser *Chicago* and two U.S. destroyers, under Rear-Admiral J. C. Crace R.N., was to join Fletcher in the Coral Sea by 4 May. Nimitz gave Fletcher overall command, instructed him to 'destroy enemy ships, shipping and aircraft at favorable opportunities in order to assist in checking further advance by enemy in the New Guinea-Solomons Area' and, with marvellous reliance on the man on the spot, left the rest up to him.

Fletcher's carriers mustered between them forty-two Grumman 4F4 Martlet fighters, seventy-four Douglas SBD Dauntless dive-bombers, and twenty-five Douglas TBD Devastator torpedo-bombers. Both these bomber types were by then obsolescent, but *Yorktown* was comparatively new, having been completed in 1938. *Lexington* was a veteran, completed in 1927 but recently modernized. Some of her crew had been on board since first commissioning and, with previous success under their belts, her air group was probably the most confident in the U.S. Navy. For the Japanese, Takagi's carrier admiral Rear-Admiral Tadaichi Hara had forty-two Zekes, forty-one Vals, and forty-two Kates. Most of the aircrew were veterans but there was already a slight but ominous dilution of skill; Japan was already having some difficulty replacing experienced aircrew.

Fletcher's two task forces met on 1 May, about 250 miles south-west of Espiritu Santo, and at once began to fuel. As usual in Fletcher's forces, fuelling was rather leisurely. Fitch had not finished next day, so Fletcher set off westward in *Yorktown* alone to look for the Japanese, thus splitting his force in the likely presence of the enemy. On the evening of 3 May Fletcher heard of the Japanese landing at Tulagi and made a rapid run northwards through the night to begin flying off the first of three strikes before dawn on the 4th. *Yorktown*'s SBDs and TBDs expended twenty-two torpedoes, seventy-six 1,000-lb bombs and 83,000 rounds of machine-gun bullets to sink a handful of small vessels, none bigger than a minesweeper, a result which Nimitz later called 'disappointing in terms of ammunition expended to results obtained'. However, *Yorktown*'s aircrew believed, and claimed, much greater results at the time, and Task Force 17 returned in very good spirits to meet Fitch and Crace the next day, 5 May, and, once again, refuel.

Takagi's force entered the Coral Sea from the north that very day, and early on 6 May *Zuikaku* and *Shokaku* were only some seventy miles north of *Yorktown* and *Lexington*, who were then, with the rest of Fletcher's ships, refuelling in the open, under a clear, brilliant sky. Inexplicably, Hara had ordered no air searches to the south-east that morning, while Fletcher's searches stopped short of Hara's ships, which were then hidden under thick cloud overcast. So an excellent chance for a carrier battle, on terms favourable to him, passed Takagi by. After fuelling, the oiler *Neosho* and her attendant destroyer *Sims* were detached to steam southwards to the next fuelling rendezvous.

Above: Vice-Admiral Frank J. Fletcher U.S.N.

Right: 'Lady Lex'—one of the U.S. Navy's best-loved ships, the carrier *Lexington*

Below: A score for Lady Lex's fighter pilots—one Zeke beached on a coral reef

Coral Sea, approximately
1100 hours, 8 May 1942. The
Japanese carrier *Shokaku* under
heavy dive-bomber and torpedo
attack by aircraft from *Yorktown*

Unwittingly, *Neosho* and *Sims* provided the perfect decoy. They were sighted on 7 May by one of Hara's reconnaissance planes, which reported them as 'a carrier and a cruiser'. Delighted to find his enemy at last, Hara launched a bomb and torpedo strike at maximum strength, thus committing his main force to a very minor target. *Sims* was sunk and *Neosho*, because of a navigational error, drifted for four days before being sighted and scuttled by a torpedo from a U.S. destroyer.

Meanwhile, Fletcher dispatched Crace's force westwards to attack the Port Moresby Invasion Group, which had been reported nearing the Jomard Passage. By so doing Fletcher weakened his own anti-aircraft gun screen and, of course, deprived Crace's ships of air cover. Crace's force was duly attacked by aircraft from Rabaul and also, incidentally, by U.S.A.A.F. aircraft from Australia. After undergoing and surviving an air attack as severe as that which had sunk *Prince of Wales* and *Repulse*, Crace's force disengaged to the south when, some time later, the invasion group was reported to have retired.

Crace's force, too, had been an ideal decoy. Just as *Sims* and *Neosho* had drawn off Hara's main assault, so Crace had diverted the land-based aircraft attack from Rabaul. Plotters at Pearl Harbor could see a perfect situation for Fletcher developing on the operations board—both threats temporarily removed, allowing him to get at the Port Moresby Invasion Group unmolested. Shortly after Crace had been detached, one of *Yorktown*'s planes reported sighting 'two carriers and four heavy cruisers'. Fletcher naturally assumed this must be Takagi's striking force and, without further verification, launched a strike of ninety-three aircraft. But when the aircraft returned it was found that there had been a decoding error: the message should have read 'two heavy cruisers and two destroyers'. So Fletcher had also committed his maximum force to a subsidiary target. Bravely, he allowed the strike to go on and once more his incredible luck held. The strike

were passing off the Louisiades, flying through cloud and mist at 15,000 feet when, by the greatest good luck, one of *Lexington*'s most experienced pilots, Commander W. B. Ault, sighted a carrier and other ships almost thirty miles away in clearer weather to starboard. This was Goto's force, and the carrier was *Shoho*. Despite opposition from *Shoho*'s Zekes, the two air groups overpowered *Shoho* with thirteen bomb and seven torpedo hits. She sank at 11.33 a.m. and listeners in *Lexington* and *Yorktown*'s operations rooms heard the exultant voice of Lieutenant Commander R. E. Dixon, leading one of *Lexington*'s Dauntless squadrons, calling out loud and clear: 'Scratch one flat-top, Dixon to Carrier, scratch one flat-top!' It was Japan's first carrier loss of the war, and a great moment for the Allied ships.

Lexington and *Yorktown* were ready to launch another strike that afternoon, but Fletcher wisely decided against it. He did not know where Takagi's carriers were, and with the weather worsening there was hardly time to launch and recover in daylight even if they were found. Fletcher headed westwards, hoping to catch the Port Moresby Invasion Group the next morning, 8 May.

It was by no means too late for Takagi. He now had a good idea of Fletcher's whereabouts, and his aircrews were itching to attack, after a very frustrating period for them. Hara so far had nothing but blunders and omissions to show for his part. At 4.30 p.m. a strike of twelve bombers and fifteen torpedo-bombers was launched, but in squally weather they missed their targets and, ironically, had jettisoned their bombs and torpedoes when they inadvertently found Fletcher's ships by flying right over them. Nine Japanese aircraft were shot down in dog-fights with Wildcats. Three actually tried to land on *Yorktown*, mistaking her for *Shokaku*. More were lost while trying to find and land on their carriers and eventually only six of the twenty-seven aircraft of that strike survived.

Both fleet commanders considered, and rejected, plans for a surface action that night. The main battle therefore took place the next day, 8 May, with carrier strike and counter-strike. Fletcher was now well on into the Coral Sea, in exactly the position the Japanese had hoped to catch him. But by now one arm of the pincer, *Shoho*, had gone, and Hara's air groups had suffered losses. Both sides could muster about 120 aircraft, although the balance of combat experience still rested with the Japanese. Inouye had already ordered the invasion force to withdraw, after he had heard of *Shoho*'s loss and the presence of Crace's ships, but it was still possible for them to return, if Hara's pilots could pull it off.

Both sides flew searches before dawn and sighted each other at about the same time. Hara gained time by launching his strike without waiting for an exact sighting report, but the Americans were the first actually to attack, arriving over Takagi's force just before 11 a.m. *Zuikaku* happened to be hidden under cloud and the main attack fell upon *Shokaku*. More than twenty of the

The end of 'Lady Lex'

Right: A huge explosion, probably of gasoline, on board *Lexington*
Far right: Lady Lex, still operating aircraft after two bomb and two torpedo hits from Japanese aircraft, approximately 1500 hours, 8 May 1942
Below: The end of *Lexington*. Ships gather round her to take off survivors

bombers failed to find the enemy at all and the torpedo-bombers released their torpedoes at too great a range, so that they were easily evaded. But *Yorktown*'s dive-bombers scored two hits on *Shokaku* and *Lexington*'s one. The big carrier was set on fire forward so that she could land on aircraft but not launch. Many of her aircraft were transferred to *Zuikaku* and Takagi ordered her to head for home shortly after 1 p.m. She reached Truk, and eventually Japan, after an exciting passage in which she nearly capsized.

Takagi had let *Shokaku* go because by that time he thought that both American carriers had been sunk. Hara's strike, of eighteen Zekes, thirty-three Vals and eighteen torpedo Kates, found *Yorktown* and *Lexington* in bright sunshine, with visibility unlimited. Now, at last, the Japanese pilots had the targets they had longed for. *Yorktown* was hit by one bomb forward, which did no serious damage, and managed to dodge several torpedoes. *Lexington* was hit by two torpedoes and two bombs, but the fires were put out, the list corrected by counter-flooding, and the ship seemed safe.

Japanese aircrew were as prone to exaggeration as the Americans, and Hara's pilots returned claiming to have sunk two American carriers. They were half right. Often in the Pacific, a carrier survived the initial damage only to succumb to later fires and explosions. So it was with *Lexington*. At 12.47 p.m. there was an explosion caused by an electrical spark igniting petrol vapour. This was followed by a second explosion and more fierce fires and at 5.10 *Lexington* had to be abandoned, to be sunk at 8 p.m. by a torpedo from a destroyer.

Yamamoto ordered Takagi to return to the battle, but Fletcher had withdrawn. Curiously enough, the Port Moresby Invasion Group could now have turned round and made their landing with every chance of success. Their only opposition would have been land-based aircraft, which had already shown their fallibility in attacking ships. But the invasion force also retired. The battle was over.

So ended the Battle of the Coral Sea. It was the first in naval history in which no ship on either side ever caught sight of an enemy ship, the whole action being fought by aircraft. Tactically, the Japanese had gained another victory. *Shoho* was a fair exchange for *Sims*, *Neosho* and 'Lady Lex'. However, *Shokaku* was badly damaged and *Zuikaku*'s air group had suffered losses, so that neither carrier could be present at Midway, when either or both might very well have turned the battle in Japan's favour.

At Pearl Harbor, there was grief over the loss of *Lexington*, but Coral Sea was very soon perceived as the strategic victory it was. For the first time in the war, Japan's invasion plans had been upset and her invasion force had been made to turn back. The effect on Allied morale was enormous. So the Japanese were not invincible after all.

48   Still smiling—*Lexington* survivors being hauled to safety

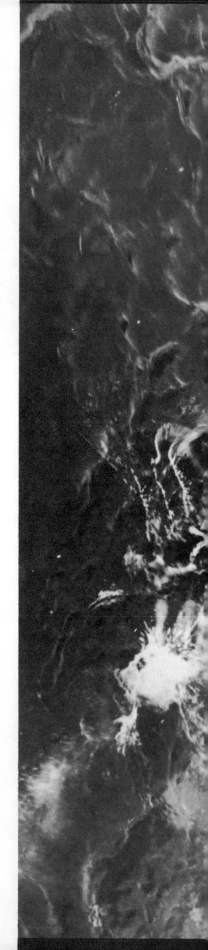

4 MIDWAY

The Japanese High Command were not too dismayed at the outcome of the battle in the Coral Sea. It was a temporary eddy in the tide of victory. On 5 May, while the battle was still in progress, Imperial Japanese Headquarters gave Yamamoto a directive to carry out Operation MI, the invasion and occupation of Midway Island and the western Aleutians, the date for the invasion of Midway being the night of 5/6 June. Midway would give the Japanese an advanced warning and defence post at the western end of the Hawaiian chain, while the Aleutians would pin down the northern end of the Japanese defence line. More important to Yamamoto, a move against Midway would surely bring about a confrontation with the U.S. fleet.

Yamamoto's desire for one great decisive, 'show-down' battle with the U.S. fleet was strategically sound. If the American fleet were decisively defeated, Hawaii would fall, and the Japanese would be able to roll back the war to the shores of America, which were very inadequately defended. In such circumstances, the American people would hardly have agreed to concentrate upon the war against Germany—not with a treacherous enemy of their own off their western coast. A Second Front could not then have been mounted until the United States had settled with Japan, by which time Russia might have defeated Germany on her own, with such assistance as Great Britain could afford. The Iron Curtain would not then have stopped at the Elbe, but at the Rhine, possibly even at Calais.

But success led Yamamoto to neglect basic rules of naval warfare. At the very time when he could have brought about the decisive battle he longed for, he chose to disperse his ships to pursue different objectives. He could have drawn up his huge armada of eight carriers, with their 400 aircraft, eleven battleships, thirteen heavy cruisers, eleven light cruisers and over sixty destroyers, and advanced upon Midway. Nimitz would have had to give battle with what ships he had, as indeed he did, and Yamamoto's fleet should have been more than strong enough to win.

But, once again, that was not the Japanese way. Instead, Yamamoto and his staff prepared a characteristically labyrinthine Japanese plan, including a diversionary decoy and a pincer movement, and involving no less than five major forces, some of which were themselves further divided into two, three or even four subdivisions. An advance expeditionary force of submarines was spread out in a line to report the movements of the American fleet when, as Yamamoto expected, it sallied forth from Pearl Harbor after receiving the news that Midway was under attack. The Carrier Striking Force, once again under Nagumo flying his flag in *Akagi*, with *Kaga*, *Hiryu* and *Soryu*, would strike first at Midway and then at the American fleet when it arrived. The Midway Occupation Force was commanded by Vice-Admiral Nobutake Kondo, and consisted of a covering group, with battle-

Previous pages: *Yorktown* being hit by Lieutenant Joichi Tomanaga's torpedo-bomber, 4 June 1942. *Yorktown* eventually sank on 6 June

ships and cruisers, a close support group of cruisers and destroyers, a transport group under Rear-Admiral Raizo Tanaka of transports and freighters screened by destroyers, a seaplane group to set up a base at Kure Island, and a minesweeping group. Yamamoto himself commanded the main body, with three battleships, one of them Yamamoto's flagship, the 60,000-ton, 18-inch gunned monster *Yamato*, and the light carrier *Hosho*. Four of the main body's battleships were detached to cover the Northern Area Force, under Vice-Admiral Boshiro Hosogaya, with its own carriers and cruisers, to invade the Aleutian islands of Adak, Attu and Kiska. The Aleutian attack was the diversionary decoy which would, Yamamoto hoped, at least distract attention and at best divert powerful American forces northwards, away from the main action.

The plan was for Nagumo's carriers to strike at Midway. When the American fleet came out, Yamamoto's battleships would close them. The American ships would then be crushed in the triple pincers of Nagumo's carriers, Yamamoto's battleships and Kondo's battleships from the Midway Occupation Force. It was curious that Yamamoto, the most enlightened advocate of carrier warfare, should still place such emphasis on destroying his enemy with heavy guns. The battleships would have been far better employed in close support of the carriers. The two light carriers *Ryujo* and *Junyo*, far north off the Aleutians, would have been better employed under Nagumo.

The other major weakness in Yamamoto's planning was excusable. Unaware that the Japanese codes had been broken, he was sure that the American fleet would not sail from Pearl Harbor until the first news that Midway was threatened. Japanese aircrew reports from the Coral Sea indicated that both American carriers had either been sunk or so badly damaged they could not take part, even if the American fleet did put to sea. In short, Yamamoto planned in the belief that it was virtually impossible for the American carriers to be anywhere near Midway when he attacked it. Ironically, Japanese war games had suggested a situation in which American carriers might appear on Nagumo's flank while he was striking Midway—exactly as it happened in the battle. Rear-Admiral Ugaki, Yamamoto's chief of staff, who had already somewhat arbitrarily weighted the games in the carriers' favour, brushed the question aside.

In fact, Nimitz and his staff already knew in considerable detail of Yamamoto's plans, his targets and the likeliest dates. Nimitz himself was always unshakably convinced that Yamamoto's objective was Midway. With such accurate prior information, Nimitz was able to beat Yamamoto to every conclusion. When the Japanese submarines, for example, formed their patrol line on 3 June, the American ships were already well past them. The submarines saw nothing throughout the whole battle.

The U.S. fleet had sailed in two task forces on 28 and 30 May

Left: Admiral Chester W. Nimitz, C-in-C Pacific Fleet, inspecting the garrison of Midway Island

53

and included *Yorktown*, whose bomb damage at the Coral Sea
had been repaired by the dockyard at Pearl in two days (Admiral
Fitch had estimated ninety). Besides *Yorktown*, Nimitz had at his
disposal *Enterprise*, his most experienced carrier, and *Hornet*, who
was still comparatively new to Pacific battle, with a total of some
230 aircraft, thirteen cruisers and about thirty destroyers. On
Midway Island itself, where the ground defences had been
strengthened as much as possible in the previous few weeks, there
was a heterogeneous collection of about 150 aircraft, from B-17
Flying Fortresses to ancient Brewster Buffalo fighters, and
including six of the new Grumman Avenger TBRs, which would
replace the Devastator in the fleet.

As for the Coral Sea, Nimitz divided his ships into two groups.
TF 16, with *Enterprise* and *Hornet*, was to have been commanded
by Halsey, but he had already had an energetic war and was
suffering from a debilitating skin disease. He was replaced for the
operation by Rear-Admiral Raymond Spruance, who could not
have been a greater contrast in manner to Halsey: quiet where
Halsey was forthright, shunning personal publicity where Halsey
was a war correspondent's dream, a shy, thoughtful, ascetic man
who ate and drank frugally. Bold yet wary in action, he was

capable of thinking clearly under the greatest stress, and in time he emerged as the greatest sea-captain in the Pacific, who went on winning battles for his country. TF 17, with *Yorktown*, was commanded by Fletcher, who was senior to Spruance and had overall command. Nimitz still had some battleships but they were too slow to keep up with the carriers and would themselves need air cover, so he kept them off the west coast of America, as he had done at the time of the Coral Sea action.

After fuelling, Spruance and Fletcher met on 2 June about 325 miles north-east of Midway, a carefully chosen position where the carriers could lie undetected, whilst long-range 700-mile searches from Midway could look for the Japanese fleet. Nimitz sent five cruisers and thirteen destroyers north to engage Hosogaya's Aleutian Attack Force. He had now done all he could: he had his maximum strength in the optimum position for its use. Events must now wait on the Japanese.

The component parts of Yamamoto's complicated scheme sailed from various ports in Japan and the Marianas at the end of May and by 1 June they were all steaming eastwards through fog, rain and high winds. On the 3rd and 4th aircraft from *Ryujo* and *Junyo* attacked Dutch Harbor in the Aleutians. The islands were lightly defended and the Japanese were eventually able to land and occupy Attu and Kiska islands, after some minor naval engagements and strenuous counter-attacks by the U.S.A.A.F.

In some American minds, the loss of these admittedly insignificant islands slightly tarnished the great victory to come. But Nimitz was not to be drawn into what he knew was only a side show. The vital battle would be fought round Midway and this opened shortly before 9 a.m. on 3 June when the pilot of a Catalina at the end of his patrol 'leg', some 700 miles out from Midway, sighted what he took to be the main Japanese fleet, about thirty miles ahead. 'Do you see what I see?' he asked his co-pilot. 'You're damned right I do!' came the reply. They tracked the ships, which were part of the Midway Occupation Force, until 11 a.m., when they reported 'eleven enemy ships, steering east, at 19 knots'.

A strike of nine B-17 bombers from Midway found the ships at about 4.30 that afternoon and made three high-level bombing attacks. They claimed to have damaged 'two battleships or heavy cruisers' but actually they obtained no hits. Four Catalinas armed with torpedoes had slightly better luck in a moonlight attack by radar at about 1.30 a.m. the next morning. They hit one tanker and caused some damage and casualties, although the ship was able to steam on. This was the only success by any shore-based aircraft in the battle, although they were to have an important diversionary effect at a crucial time.

Nimitz and Fletcher knew from decoded signals that this force could not be their main opponent. Nagumo's carriers had to be much closer, probably not more than 400 miles west of Midway.

Douglas Devastator torpedo-
bombers ranged on the flight
deck of *Enterprise.* Only four of
these aircraft survived the
battle for Midway

At 7.50 in the evening of 3 June, Fletcher altered course to steer
south-west, aiming to be about 200 miles north of Midway by
dawn on the 4th, in position to fly off strikes against Nagumo as
soon as he was found. At the same time, Nagumo was steering
south-west at 25 knots through the night, so as to be in position
to strike at Midway soon after dawn. So the two carrier forces
were converging upon each other, for a confrontation some time
on 4 June. The only difference was that Fletcher could guess
where his enemy was, while Nagumo did not even suspect that
his opponent was at sea.

Thursday, 4 June, dawned bright and clear for the Americans,
with visibility up to 40 miles and a light south-easterly trade wind
blowing, which dropped away as the sun came up at 4.30. *Yorktown*
launched search planes to cover a northern semi-circle up to 100
miles in radius, just at the time when Nagumo, about 215 miles
to the west, was launching his first strike against Midway.
Nagumo's ships were still shrouded in the cloud cover of the cold
front which had hidden them for some days, but they were sighted
and the eagerly expected message arrived at 5.34 a.m.: 'Enemy
carriers'. The message was intercepted from a Catalina transmit-
ting to Midway. Nine minutes later, the Catalina reported 'Many
enemy planes heading Midway bearing 320° distant 160'. Shortly
after 6 a.m. the same aircraft reported 'two carriers and battleships bearing 320°, 180 miles from Midway, course 135°, speed

25'. This position, about 200 miles west-south-west of TF 16, was the first firm news about Nagumo's carriers. Fletcher chose to recover his search aircraft and await more intelligence before launching *Yorktown*'s strike. He ordered Spruance to 'proceed southwesterly and attack enemy carriers when definitely located' and said he would follow himself as soon as his aircraft had been recovered.

Meanwhile, Nagumo's strike of thirty-six Kates and thirty-six Vals, escorted by thirty-six Zekes and led by Lieutenant Tomonaga of *Hiryu*, were on their way to Midway, where they arrived at about 6.30. They bombed buildings, hangars, oil storage tanks and the hospital, but they did not put the runways out of action and killed very few people on the ground. The Marine fighters did their best but the antique Buffaloes and the Wildcats were hopelessly outclassed, and seventeen were shot down. However, they and the Midway gunners shot down about a third of the strike, which was very good going indeed, and, more important, Midway had survived the attack.

Midway also tried to strike back at Nagumo. Warned by radar, six Avengers and four B-26 Marauders of the U.S.A.A.F. took off at 6.15 and reached the Japanese fleet at about 7.10. Unescorted by fighters of their own, the bombers were severely handled by the carriers' Zekes; only two Marauders and one of the Avengers, and that badly shot up, returned to Midway. None of them

scored any hits on any Japanese ship. However, their attack was most fortunate in the end. Tomonaga had come back from Midway, reporting that another strike was needed. These attacks by Midway bombers proved him right. It was at this point, when Nagumo had to make a series of crucial decisions, that things began to go wrong, for him and for Japan.

The Japanese had begun to fly off searches by seaplanes from the cruisers at 4.35 that morning. Nagumo had kept back a full strike of ninety-three aircraft, armed with torpedoes and bombs, to deal with any enemy ships sighted. Three float-planes took off smartly, but the fourth, from the cruiser *Tone*, was delayed until 5 a.m. By seven o'clock, when Nagumo learned from Tomonaga that Midway needed another strike, he had still heard nothing from any of the searching float-planes. So, at 7.15, he ordered the ranks of waiting aircraft to be broken up and the aircraft to be struck down into the hangars below, while the Midway strike landed on. He also ordered the Kates that had been armed with torpedoes—for use against ships—to be rearmed with bombs—for bombing Midway Atoll. This was an evolution which would take at least an hour.

It was an ill-chance for the Japanese that the U.S. fleet should happen to be in the search sector covered by the delayed plane from *Tone*. At 7.28 the first message arrived from this plane: 'Ten enemy surface ships, in position 10° Midway, distance 240 miles, course 150°, speed over 20 knots.' There was no mention of carriers, but this was the first inkling Nagumo had that he might have opposition. But ten ships 200 miles away did not worry him and he did not cancel his order to break up the strike. In any case, he had to keep decks clear for the returning Midway strike.

But something must have snagged in Nagumo's cautious mind, or perhaps it was the advice of one of his staff, for at 7.45 he changed his mind. He gave the order 'Prepare to attack enemy fleet units' and 'leave torpedoes on those aircraft not yet changed to bombs'. At 7.47 he signalled to *Tone*'s maddeningly deliberate pilot to 'Ascertain ship types and maintain contact'. At 8.09 a.m. the pilot replied: 'Five cruisers and five destroyers.' But, at 8.20, there came the addition which changed the whole picture of the battle for Nagumo. 'Enemy is accompanied by what appears to be a carrier.'

This message could not have come at a worse time for Nagumo. Some of his aircraft were still on deck, some struck below in the hangars, some still armed with torpedoes, some with bombs, while the incoming Midway strike still had to be landed on. Rear-Admiral Yamaguchi on *Hiryu*, a most able officer, suggested at least his ship's strike should be flown off to attack the American ships. Nagumo rejected the suggestion, which was a good one, and might well have caught Spruance still closing his target. He ordered all aircraft to be struck down and the returning aircraft landed on.

It was difficult for Nagumo to make the right decision because he was harried at every turn. His fighters were at that moment beating off another attack from Midway, and if he had launched a strike it would have had no escort. The Marines and U.S.A.A.F. on Midway had attacked with Devastators, Flying Fortresses (which had taken off before dawn) and Vindicators. Several aircraft were lost, for near-misses on *Hiryu* and *Akagi*, but they did serve to keep Nagumo preoccupied at a critical time. The U.S. submarine *Nautilus* added to the confusion by attacking a battle-ship and evading the subsequent depth-charge attack.

The Midway strike had been recovered by 9.18, and all four Japanese carriers at once began furiously to refuel, rearm and range up a full strike against the American carrier, or carriers.

Spruance by now had the information that his opponent was some 200 miles west-south-west of Midway and he coolly calcu-lated that the best time to attack would be when Nagumo was just recovering his Midway strike and his decks were hampered by landing aircraft. Spruance also decided that his would be an 'all-out effort' using every available aircraft except those needed for protecting his own ships, even if that meant that the first aircraft off had to orbit for an hour while the second group was ranged up and launched.

The first of TF 16's strike of sixty-seven Dauntless dive-bombers,

Midway, approximately 1100 hours, 4 June 1942. U.S. Navy SBD Dauntlesses over a burning Japanese carrier

twenty-nine Devastator torpedo-bombers and twenty Wildcat
fighters took off at 7.02. But the strike was not the heavy combined
blow Spruance had intended. A Japanese reconnaissance plane
was seen circling on the horizon. TF 16 had been sighted and so
Enterprise's Dauntlesses, led by Lieutenant-Commander McClusky,
were ordered to go on at once without waiting for the rest, and
they took departure at 7.52. The rest formed up in some confusion,
Enterprise's fighters mistakenly taking station above *Hornet*'s
Devastators, leaving their own Devastators unescorted. *Hornet*'s
fighters lost their Devastators and flew with their Dauntlesses
instead. Thus the strike flew in four separate groups: *Enterprise*'s
dive-bombers, *Hornet*'s dive-bombers and the fighters, followed by
the two Devastator torpedo-bomber squadrons.

Nagumo had steamed north-east to close the distance while
ranging up his next strike, so that when the first of TF 16's aircraft
arrived at his reported position, the sea was empty. *Hornet*'s
dive-bombers and fighters turned south-east to search, and found
nothing. The dive-bombers returned to their ship or to Midway,
while the fighters ran out of fuel and ditched. The two torpedo-
bomber squadrons turned north and, just after 9.30, sighted the
Japanese fleet.

The two Devastator squadron commanders, Waldron of *Hornet*
and Lindsey of *Enterprise*, knew very well how vulnerable their
aircraft would be without close fighter support. Waldron wrote
before the battle: 'My greatest hope is that we encounter a
favorable tactical situation, but if we don't, and the worst comes
to the worst, I want each of us to do his utmost to destroy our
enemies. If there is only one plane left to make a final run in, I
want that man to go in and get a hit. May God be with us all.'[14]

In the event the tactical situation could not have been less favourable, and the worst did come to the worst. Skimming low and slow over the sea, with no fighter escort, the Devastators were sitting ducks for the attacking Zekes. All Waldron's squadron were shot down. Only one man, Ensign Gay, survived by clinging to a rubber seat cushion and ducking underwater whenever strafing Zekes passed overhead. Ten of Lindsey's were shot down, and no hit was scored on any Japanese ship.

However, the Devastator's sacrifice was not in vain. They provided the perfect decoy. While the Zekes had been drawn down to sea-level to attack them, the dive-bombers from *Enterprise* and *Yorktown*, which had flown off an hour later, met over the Japanese fleet. After finding nothing where he had expected to see the enemy, McClusky had turned north and soon sighted the destroyer *Arashi*, steaming to rejoin the main fleet. *Arashi* obligingly led the dive-bombers to the carriers.

The timing was perfect. The Japanese aircraft had been rearmed and ranged up. All four carriers had evaded the torpedo attacks and were racing up into wind to launch their aircraft, their flight decks crowded, when the dive-bombers struck. From 15,000 feet above, the Japanese carriers appeared as long, bright yellow rectangles, each with a fifty-foot red disc painted forward. McClusky's two squadrons began their dives at about 10.25. As one pilot, Lieutenant Dickinson, said, 'the target was utterly satisfying. The squadron's dive was perfect. This was the absolute. After this, I felt, anything would be just anticlimax'.[15]

Akagi was hit by three bombs, the second of which penetrated to the hangar and exploded, setting off sympathetic explosions in the torpedoes stored there. Great fires broke out, fed by petrol

The loss of 'Yorktown'

Above: Damage-control parties working to repair the flight deck. *Yorktown* was able to recover and launch aircraft within two hours
Right: *Yorktown*'s flight deck after the first Japanese attack, 1300 hours, 4 June 1942
Below: The U.S. destroyer *Hammann* preparing to come alongside the crippled and listing *Yorktown*
Below right: *Yorktown* belches smoke after suffering three bomb hits during the first Japanese air attack

and spread by more bomb and torpedo explosions. Nagumo and
his staff were soon forced to transfer to a cruiser. They left *Akagi* in
a state, as Nagumo's chief of staff said, 'just like hell!' Her
crew abandoned her at 7.15 that evening, but she floated until
just before dawn, when she was dispatched by a Japanese
destroyer's torpedo.

Kaga was hit four times, one bomb demolishing the bridge,
killing the captain and everybody on it, with the same fatal
sequence of fire and explosions. She too was abandoned and
broke in two after an enormous internal explosion at about 7.30
that evening. *Yorktown*'s bombers dived on *Soryu* and scored three
hits. Within twenty minutes, fires and explosions forced her to be
abandoned and she sank, on fire from end to end after three
torpedo hits by *Nautilus*, at about the same time as *Kaga*.

Hiryu, some way ahead of the others, alone escaped and
launched two strikes of eighteen Vals, ten Kates and twelve
Zekes. Some of them were shot down, but shortly before noon
the first of them reached *Yorktown* and hit her with three bombs
and two torpedoes. The ship was crippled and came to a standstill.
Her crew abandoned her that afternoon just as ten of her
Dauntlesses, transferred to *Enterprise*, were getting revenge for her
by taking part in a strike on *Hiryu* which obtained four hits. *Hiryu*
went the way of her three sisters, although she survived for some
time; her crew abandoned her at 3.30 the next morning, and
Japanese destroyers torpedoed her. But it was 9 a.m. before she
finally sank, taking with her Rear-Admiral Yamaguchi.

Yamamoto was slow to realize the disaster that had overtaken
Japan. That evening he was steaming up in *Yamato* from the
west, still anticipating a major gun action. But Spruance, cautious
when caution was needed, had cannily retired to the east and was
not to be drawn, although the cruiser *Mikuma* was sunk by
Enterprise's aircraft on the 6th. In the early hours of 5 June,
Yamamoto finally awoke to the catastrophe which had befallen
the Japanese Navy and ordered a general retreat. *Yorktown* stayed
afloat, and men were put back on board her, she was taken in
tow, and there seemed a chance of saving her. But in the early
afternoon of 6 June, the Japanese submarine I.168 found her, and
put two torpedoes into her and one into the destroyer *Hammann*
alongside her. *Yorktown* finally rolled over and sank at 6 a.m.
on the 7th.

The loss of *Yorktown* was the final act in the battle of Midway.
Like Waterloo, it had been a 'damned close run thing'. One
signal misplaced, one float-plane taking off on time, one more
observant pilot, one accident of timing favourable to Japan, might
have made all the difference. But Spruance had taken his chance
when it was given him. He had struck at the right time, with the
right weapon in the right place. The U.S. Navy, with the men
on Midway Atoll itself, had together won a strategic victory
equal to Salamis, Lepanto or Trafalgar.

5 GUADALCANAL

The first American landing on foreign soil since 1898—U.S. Marines going ashore on Guadalcanal, August 1942

The victory at Midway, coming as it did like a flash of light and hope for the Allies at a very gloomy time, promoted consideration of some kind of defensive counter-attack in the Coral Sea area. The debate was complicated by the fact that this area was in General MacArthur's South-west Pacific Command, while the troops, ships, and transports needed for such a campaign were administered by Admiral Nimitz's Pacific Ocean Area. MacArthur proposed a direct frontal assault upon Rabaul, in New Britain. Admiral Nimitz demurred: he was reluctant to commit his ships, and especially his few and precious remaining carriers, to such a venture. A compromise was reached. Vice-Admiral R. L. Ghormley, C.-in-C. South Pacific Area under Nimitz, would command an assault on the Santa Cruz Islands and the seaplane base at Tulagi. When a satisfactory base had been established, command would be transferred to MacArthur, who would direct a dual assault through Papua and the Solomons, to converge eventually upon Rabaul. The demarcation line between Nimitz's and MacArthur's areas was shifted one degree west to admit the targets to Nimitz's command.

Plans were well advanced for Operation WATCHTOWER, as it was called, when reconnaissance planes and coast-watchers reported the disturbing news that the Japanese were building an airstrip on a grassy plain on the north coast of an island called Guadalcanal. It was, in fact, one of the only places suitable for an airbase in the whole of the mountainous, jungle-clad Solomon Islands chain, and, as such, it was strategically priceless. Previous planning was abandoned. Everything was concentrated upon Guadalcanal, with a target date for the landing of 1 August 1942.

Guadalcanal was a planner's nightmare. There were no proper maps or charts. Irrevocable decisions had to be made on incomplete data. The Allied command structure was clumsily improvised. General Vandegrift, whose 1st U.S. Marine Division were to make the landing, asked for a postponement. But Admiral King would only agree to put the date back seven days. So, on 7 August, preceded by cruiser and destroyer bombardment from Fire Support Groups and covered by aircraft from *Saratoga*, *Enterprise* and *Wasp* (newly arrived from the Atlantic) in Admiral Fletcher's task force west of Guadalcanal, the Marines went ashore on Tulagi and Guadalcanal, in the first landing by U.S. troops on foreign soil since 1898. The Tulagi assault met fanatical resistance from the Japanese garrison (a foretaste of things to come) but the Guadalcanal landing, on the north coast, east of Lunga Point, was unopposed, which was as well, for the manner and organization of the landing left much room for improvement. In thirty-six hours the Marines had taken the airstrip and named it Henderson Field, after Major Lofton R. Henderson, U.S. Marine Corps, who had died leading a bombing attack from Midway on *Hiryu* on 4 June. In the next six months, the struggle for Guadalcanal was virtually to mean the battle for Henderson.

67

The Japanese had been taken unawares by the landings, but their naval reaction was swift and savage. Vice-Admiral Gunichi Mikawa, flying his flag in the heavy cruiser *Chokai*, with the heavy cruisers *Aoba*, *Kako*, *Kinugasa* and *Furutaka*, the light cruisers *Tenryu* and *Yubari*, and the destroyer *Yunagi*, sailed from Rabaul on 7 August. He was reported, twice, off Bougainville the next day, but the messages were relayed in such a way as to cause no alarm at Guadalcanal. Mikawa's own reconnaissance aircraft told him what he wanted to know: fifteen transports off Guadalcanal, three off Tulagi, escorted by cruisers and destroyers and, one report said, a battleship. In spite of the battleship, Mikawa decided to attack on the night of the 8th/9th. His ships were trained for night action. They had no radar, but abnormally gifted night lookouts. They had the Long Lance torpedo and searchlight batteries whose controls were linked to the main gun armaments. By night, Mikawa was confident of the outcome.

Meanwhile, on the Allied side, everything was peaceful. Nobody suspected an imminent attack. A Southern Group, consisting of the cruisers H.M.A.S. *Australia* (flagship of Rear-Admiral V. A. C. Crutchley, V.C., R.N.), H.M.A.S. *Hobart*, and U.S.S. *Chicago*, with the U.S. destroyers *Patterson* and *Bagley*, were allocated the south channel, between Guadalcanal and the small, hump-backed jungly island of Savo. A Northern Group of the U.S. cruisers *Vincennes*, *Quincy* and *Astoria*, with the U.S. destroyers *Helm* and *Wilson*, patrolled the channel north and east of Savo. Two radar-equipped destroyers watched the approaches to Savo, *Blue* to the south and *Ralph Talbot* to the north.

On the evening of 8 August Admiral Crutchley was summoned urgently to a conference with Rear-Admiral Kelly Turner, commander of the amphibious force, and Vandegrift in Turner's flagship *McCawley* lying among the transports in Lunga Roads. The three commanders had to debate a most alarming development: Fletcher had been complaining that his ships were short of fuel and his fighter strength was dwindling dangerously. He had announced that he was taking his carriers away, forthwith. Crutchley had left no particular instructions with his ships in his absence. When the conference broke up after midnight and he rejoined *Australia*, such was the false confidence the Allies had been lulled into that Crutchley decided not to search for his ships in the darkness but to remain on patrol off the troop anchorage.

At 0054 on the 9th, a few minutes after Crutchley rejoined his ship, *Chokai*'s lookouts sighted *Blue*, fine on their starboard bow. *Chokai* was going at 26 knots and her bow wave was showing a great white 'bone in her teeth' but, incredibly, *Blue*'s lookouts saw nothing and her radar screen was blank. Mikawa's ships slipped by unchallenged. At 0130 *Chokai* led through the channel between Savo and Guadalcanal and sighted another destroyer, *Jarvis*, damaged in an air attack the previous day and returning to Sydney for repairs. Once again, Mikawa was unchallenged, and soon the black shapes of *Canberra* and *Chicago* could be seen in line ahead, silhouetted against the clear horizon behind them. Mikawa gave the order to attack, ships to fire independently, and they launched torpedoes at 1.38 a.m.

About five minutes later, the Japanese ships were at last sighted, by *Canberra*, *Patterson* and *Bagley* together, and the alarm was raised. But it was too late. *Canberra*'s turrets were still trained fore and aft. Illuminated by flares from Mikawa's aircraft overhead, overwhelmed by shells and one torpedo hit on the port bow, *Canberra* was crippled and came to a dead stop in the water. *Bagley* had managed to get off one salvo of torpedoes, but *Chicago*, sighting a light to seaward, steamed out towards it and took no further part.

Having demolished the Southern Group, Mikawa now stalked the Northern ships. His force had split into two columns steaming north-east, with *Furutaka* and the two light cruisers passing closer to Savo. *Vincennes* could be seen ahead with *Quincy* and *Astoria*, as the Japanese closed them from either quarter, *Chokai* to starboard, *Furutaka* to port. At 1.50 *Chokai*'s searchlights caught and held *Astoria*. One salvo set her aircraft alight, making a perfect aiming mark. *Astoria* got one hit on *Chokai* before she was smashed into a wreck by successive salvoes and, on fire from end to end, fell out of line. Ahead of *Astoria*, *Aoba*'s searchlights revealed *Quincy* with her turrets still trained fore and aft. Her upperdeck a shambles, and her port side amidships blown open by a torpedo, *Quincy* capsized and sank at 2.35 with her captain and 370 of her people.

Captain Riefkohl in *Vincennes* did not know that Crutchley was absent. *Chicago* had not raised the alarm. The thunder from the south Riefkohl put down to the Southern ships firing at aircraft. Even when *Vincennes* was lit up by a Japanese searchlight Riefkohl was convinced it was friendly and ordered it to be extinguished. *Vincennes* possibly got one hit on *Kinugasa* before she too was soon smothered under a hail of shells and torpedo hits. Most of her

Japanese Mitsubishi G4M 'Betty' bombers from Rabaul carrying out a low-level attack on Allied shipping off Guadalcanal

crew managed to abandon her before she rolled over and sank at about 3 a.m. but more than 300 died in her. *Canberra* was dispatched by an American torpedo at 8 a.m. *Astoria* lasted until noon, when she sank after one final magazine explosion.

At 2.20 Mikawa collected his ships and retired to the west, giving *Ralph Talbot* a severe hammering in passing. In a brisk action lasting fifty minutes he had inflicted a defeat on the Allies comparable to the Italian defeat at Matapan. But it could have been worse. Mikawa did not go through and attack the transports which had been his primary target, because he feared attacks by Fletcher's aircraft at first light.

Later, Yamamoto somewhat unjustly criticized Mikawa for this retirement. Mikawa was not to know, and could never have guessed, that Fletcher had actually carried out his intention of withdrawing the carriers, and the troopship anchorage was at his mercy.

Deprived of air cover, Turner hauled his ships out of the anchorage at sunset on 9 August and departed to New Caledonia, taking half the stores and food with him and leaving the Marines on their own on Guadalcanal. The Marines, convinced they had been left to die in another Bataan, set about fortifying their position round the airstrip and getting the strip ready for service. It was only 2,600 feet long and had no drainage or steel matting for taxiing, but on 20 August twelve Marine Dauntlesses and nineteen Wildcats flew in from the converted light carrier *Long Island*. These few, almost symbolic, aircraft flying into Henderson properly began the Allied counter-offensive in the East. These wings, multiplied by the thousand, would carry the Allies to Tokyo Bay.

However, this was not apparent at the time. The Japanese High Command, still preoccupied with their campaign to capture Port Moresby overland through New Guinea, were slow to realize Allied intentions on Guadalcanal. The sharp repulse, of an overconfident and undersupported attempt to take Henderson, at the Tenaru River on 21 August woke them. They began to reinforce their troops by means of what became known as the 'Tokyo Express' under Rear-Admiral Raizo Tanaka, who led swift convoys of warships and troop ships by night down from Rabaul through the 'Slot', the passage between the twin chain of the Solomon Islands. The Allies, too, were preoccupied—with Henderson—and as both sides steadily raised their stakes on Guadalcanal it was some time before the Allies realized that Guadalcanal had become a matter of prestige as much as strategy.

After a time, the American people woke up to the truth that their troops were fighting a major campaign on this hitherto unknown island. As more details became known of the Marines' ordeal on this loathsome, lethal island, where the malarial mosquito became as great a danger as the machine gun and the mortar, the question increasingly asked, in the Chief of Staff's

Opposite above: Amphtracs (amphibian tractors) coming ashore at Guadalcanal

Opposite below: Tanamboga Island in the Solomons after a strafing attack by American carrier aircraft

71

committee as well as in public, was not 'Can we win?' but 'Can we hold on?'

The answer to that lay very largely with the respective navies, as both sides sought to choke off the other's reinforcements arriving by sea. The Guadalcanal campaign involved every kind of warship, from battleships to PT boats. There were carrier engagements, and submarine attacks, and surface ship actions by night and day, and shore bombardments by heavy guns, and bombing attacks by land-based aircraft. On land, the scale of the engagements ranged from frontal attacks in regimental strength to individual patrol activity, where murderous groping in the jungle often ended in hand-to-hand combat. Guadalcanal was a whole war on its own.

Having failed at the Tenaru River, the Japanese soon tried again. Another Tokyo Express set off, escorted by Tanaka in his flagship, the light cruiser *Jintsu*, and destroyers. They were supported by a powerful fleet including *Shokaku* and *Zuikaku* north of the Solomons. When Allied intelligence reported these moves, Fletcher's TF 61, with *Saratoga*, *Enterprise* and *Wasp*, steamed to the east of the Solomons, where, on 23 August, scout planes sighted part of the Japanese fleet. Fletcher dispatched a strike of dive-bombers and torpedo aircraft but the Japanese reversed course and their ships remained hidden under low cloud and rain storms. Fletcher then detached *Wasp*'s group to refuel.

The next day the Japanese pushed forward a sacrificial decoy, the small carrier *Ryujo*, which was duly sighted and attacked. Thus Fletcher, as at the Coral Sea, had sent his main blow against a minor target, for scouts soon discovered the big carriers. Fletcher tried to divert his strike but bad communications only complicated an already confused situation. *Ryujo* was sunk, however, by bombs and one torpedo hit. *Enterprise*'s aircraft found *Shokaku* and did minor damage.

Fletcher had sent off his strike with no fighter escort. He had fifty-three fighters 'stacked' in three layers overhead waiting for the attack he knew must come. All remaining dive-bombers and torpedo aircraft had taken off, with orders to counter-attack the Japanese fleet. Meanwhile *Saratoga* and *Enterprise* waited, every gun manned and loaded, all fuel lines drained and refilled with inert gas, battened down as though against a tropical storm.

It was not long in coming. The radar screens showed swarms of hostile aircraft. The fighters rose to meet them. Fighter direction had not been polished to the standard it later achieved and there was a time of wild activity, a hubbub of shouting over the R/T, when it was impossible to tell friend from foe. All the torpedo-Kates were beaten off but some thirty Val dive-bombers arrived undetected at 18,000 feet over *Enterprise*. The fleet's anti-aircraft barrage had been reinforced by the new battleship *North Carolina* which mounted a massive battery of AA guns (a sign of the times), but nevertheless enough Vals survived to hit *Enterprise* with three

Above: The lethal, loathsome island—jungle-fighting on Guadalcanal

Right: Sick and starving Japanese soldiers captured by American troops on Guadalcanal

U.S.S. *Wasp* living (inset) and dying after torpedo attack by a Japanese submarine, 15 September 1942

bombs, two of them penetrating deep into the ship before exploding. Damage control had improved since Midway and *Enterprise* was soon able to steam at 24 knots and recover her aircraft. But her steering gear broke down and for an agonizing time she lay immobile, while the Japanese were frantically searching for her just over the horizon, before being able to get under way again and escape. *Saratoga*, who had not been attacked at all, mounted a strike which badly damaged the seaplane carrier *Chitose*. At sunset the carriers on both sides retired, thus concluding the inconclusive Battle of the Eastern Solomons. However, the most serious reverse for the Japanese happened the next day, when Marine dive-bombers from Henderson attacked and set on fire *Jintsu* and a troop transport, *Kenryu Maru* and both had to turn back. Flying Fortresses from Espiritu Santo sank the destroyer *Mutsuki* and finished off *Kenryu Maru*.

In September, every chance was taken to fly more aircraft into

Henderson, while Tanaka took every opportunity of running the Tokyo Express. Eventually a curious balance was struck. By day, Allied aircraft from the carriers and Henderson ruled. By night, initiative returned to Tanaka and the Japanese.

Another Japanese attempt to take Henderson was defeated by the Marines at the aptly-named Bloody Ridge on 12/13 September, but the Japanese continued to have success at sea, where Allied ships tended to linger too long and too carelessly in areas where Japanese submarines were known to be operating. *Saratoga* was torpedoed by I.26 on 31 August and put out of action for three months. On 7 September, I.11 near-missed *Hornet* and *North Carolina*, and on the 15th one salvo from I.19 struck a major blow: three torpedoes hit *Wasp*, which later sank, and the others sank the destroyer *O'Brien* and damaged *North Carolina*. It was no wonder that the area between San Cristobal and Espiritu Santo became known as 'Torpedo Junction'.

Likewise, the waters off Savo Island were nicknamed 'Iron-bottom Sound'. The action of 8 August had demonstrated that the Japanese were not a short-legged, shortsighted race with poor night vision and an imitative view of tactics. Off Guadalcanal the U.S. Navy were learning, as the U.S. Army had to learn against Rommel at the Kasserine Pass in Tunisia, that superior technology and an ever-improving logistical supply of weaponry were not enough against a skilful, trained and determined enemy. But lessons were rapidly learned. Groups of ships practised together, with particular attention to night-fighting. Improved radar was fitted, and combat information centres developed in command ships.

On 7 October a striking force of the cruisers *San Francisco*, *Salt Lake City*, *Boise* and *Helena*, with five destroyers, sailed from Espiritu Santo to cover another troop convoy of two transports and eight destroyer-types. The force was under Rear-Admiral Norman Scott, who had been a spectator at Savo Island and had made up his mind that the same thing should never happen to him. He had drilled his squadron, paying special attention to night encounter techniques, and had them close under firm control—perhaps too firm, as events showed.

For their part, the Japanese had at last realized the true importance of what was happening on Guadalcanal. On 9 October, General Hyakutake, commanding the 17th Army, landed on the island to take personal command of the campaign. Another large Tokyo Express of two seaplane carriers and six destroyers sailed from Rabaul, covered by the cruisers *Aoba*, *Kinugasa* and *Furutaka*, with two destroyers, under Rear-Admiral Goto. They were sighted by aircraft and reported to Scott on the 11th. That night Scott steamed at 29 knots to close Guadalcanal and intercept. His force was in single line ahead, the destroyers disposed ahead and astern of the cruisers. Scott's line was an unwieldy two and a half miles long, and the latest radar was in *Helena*, not *San Francisco*, the flagship.

At 11 p.m. that night, Scott's ships were about eight miles north of the extreme western tip of Guadalcanal, steering north-east at 20 knots. Unknowingly, Scott had achieved the perfect attacking position, having 'crossed his enemy's T'. *Helena* actually obtained a radar contact at 11.25, range fourteen miles, but did not report it. Scott did not know of *Helena's* radar contact until the enemy were within five miles of him, when he had already decided he had gone far enough to the north-east and had ordered his force to reverse course. He therefore met his enemy when his ships were changing formation, and all his carefully drilled cohesion broke down. Scott's own destroyers were actually between him and the Japanese, and when *Helena* opened fire, having sighted ships at 2,500 yards, Scott at first ordered her to stop, thinking she was firing on friendly ships.

It was the turn of the Japanese to be surprised by night.

Santa Cruz, 26 October 1942. A Nakajima B-5N2 'Kate' torpedo-bomber seen from U.S.S. *Pensacola*

76

Accustomed to having the Slot to themselves after dark, they had their turrets trained fore and aft and were hopelessly caught. When the American cruisers opened fire, they hit *Aoba*, mortally wounding Goto, damaged *Furutaka* so badly that she later sank, and sank the destroyer *Fubuki*; *Kinugasa* and one destroyer, *Hatsuyuki*, turned away from Goto to port, and escaped attack. They met and shelled the destroyer *Duncan*, who had gained a radar contact and had steamed off to the west on her own. *Duncan* was later abandoned and sunk.

Pursuing Goto to the west, *Boise* ill-advisedly switched on a searchlight, giving *Aoba* and *Kinugasa* an aiming point. Both opened fire, and *Boise* was badly damaged. After some more desultory firing, Scott broke off, at half past midnight, and re-formed his ships.

It was believed that four Japanese cruisers and four destroyers had been sunk in this action, and the Battle of Cape Esperance, as it was called, was greeted as a great victory. It was less than that, as events would show, for Scott's line-ahead formation had been clumsy and the surprised Japanese had failed to get off their Long Lance torpedoes. But still, it was a victory, showing that the Japanese were not quite so invincible by night.

However, the Japanese had successfully landed their re-inforcements, including artillery, that night and now began a programme of bombardments of Henderson. The 14-inch guns of the battleships *Kongo* and *Haruna* shelled the airfield for ninety minutes on the night of 13/14 October and only stopped because they were disconcerted by four attacking PT boats. The next night, *Chokai* and *Kinugasa* fired 752 8-inch shells at Henderson and the night after that it was the turn of cruisers *Myoko and Maya* with 800 8-inch shells. By the 16th, Japanese transports were able

Hornet on fire and sinking after two torpedo and six bomb hits and two Japanese aircraft had crashed on her deck

to unload boldly in daylight on the beaches near Tassafaronga. For the first time, Japanese strength on Guadalcanal was equal in numbers to the Marines, and they were looking forward to 'Y' Day, 22 October, when, after a week's 'softening up', Japanese troops would at last take Henderson Field.

The main Japanese fleet meanwhile lay north of the Solomons, waiting, in Yamamoto's words to 'apprehend and annihilate any powerful forces in the Solomons area' and to fly aircraft into Henderson once the field had been taken. The Combined Fleet, though at full strength, was once again deployed in extended order, in three separate groups: a striking force, under Nagumo, consisting of a carrier group, with *Shokaku* (flag), *Zuikaku* and the light carrier *Zuiho*, a cruiser and eight destroyers, and a vanguard group, sixty miles to the north, under Rear-Admiral Hiroaki Abe, with two battleships, three cruisers and destroyer escort. Over a hundred miles to the north-west was a third force under Kondo, flying his flag in the cruiser *Atago*, with two battleships, three more cruisers and the new carrier *Junyo*.

At Henderson, the Marines and the G.I.s of the 164th Americal Regiment (whose arrival on Guadalcanal Scott's force had covered on the 12th) held out far longer than the Japanese expected and, though the naval liaison officer on Guadalcanal prematurely reported the airfield captured early on the 25th, Nagumo still had to wait, while his fuel and patience dwindled. The delay enabled Rear-Admiral Thomas Kinkaid to bring his two task forces, TF 16 with *Enterprise* and TF 17 centred round *Hornet*, to a position north of the Santa Cruz Islands. Catalinas from Espiritu Santo sighted Nagumo's ships on the afternoon of the 15th and Kinkaid launched a strike, but Nagumo, still uncertain of his enemy's position, had already withdrawn. Kinkaid was in no doubt what was expected of him, having received a signal of 'ATTACK REPEAT ATTACK' from the new C.-in-C. South Pacific, Admiral Halsey. He had relieved Ghormley on 18 October, Nimitz having decided that the theatre needed more aggressive leadership.

The main battle of Santa Cruz, on 26 October, was once again a day of strike and counter-strike between carriers, in which the tactical balance went to the Japanese. *Enterprise* launched an armed reconnaissance of 16 Dauntlesses, each with a 500-lb bomb, at first light. Two of them completely surprised *Zuiho*, putting her out of action with their bombs in an unexpected and unmolested attack. Nagumo's aircraft reported the position of one American carrier at 6.58 a.m. and his strike of sixty-five aircraft, half of them Zekes, was on its way twelve minutes later. By 7.30 *Hornet* had launched a strike of fifteen Dauntlesses, six Avengers and eight Wildcats. Thirty minutes later *Enterprise* contributed three Dauntlesses, eight Avengers and eight Wildcats. These were followed a quarter of an hour later by another force of nine Dauntlesses, nine Avengers and nine Wildcats from *Hornet*. So, while the Japanese aircraft flew in one compact strike, the Americans set off in a procession. The two strikes actually passed each other on their way. Twelve Zekes peeled off and shot down four Avengers and four Wildcats from *Enterprise*, for the loss of three of their own.

When the Japanese aircraft arrived, *Enterprise* happened to be hidden in a rain squall and the attack fell upon *Hornet*, who was hit by two torpedoes, six bombs and two aircraft which made suicide crashes on her flight deck. In a few minutes, *Hornet* had lost all power and steerage way, and came to a dead stop, a blazing wreck.

Two hundred miles away to the north-west, *Hornet*'s torpedo aircraft had become separated from their group leader Lieutenant-Commander Widhelm, leading the dive-bombers, and attacked Abe's vanguard group, with no success. The survivors of *Enterprise*'s strike joined in, also with no success. *Hornet*'s second strike badly damaged the cruiser *Chikuma*, but the results generally did not match the effort involved. Widhelm's dive-bombers, however, made up for it all. Although Widhelm himself was shot down, his aircraft hit *Shokaku* with between three and six 1,000-lb bombs, preventing her operating aircraft. But her second strike, with *Zuikaku*'s, was already attacking *Enterprise*, having sensibly ignored the stricken *Hornet*. *Enterprise* had fighters in the air but for the second time that day the fighter direction organization was found wanting. *Enterprise* was hit by two bombs. Her forward lift was put out of action, but her high speed was unimpaired and she managed to avoid a determined torpedo attack. Finally, a strike from *Junyo* scored a hit on the battleship *South Dakota*, who was part of *Enterprise*'s anti-aircraft screen, and dropped one bomb clean through the hull of the cruiser *San Juan*.

Attempts to take *Hornet* in tow were abandoned. Nor could torpedoes or gunfire sink her. Eventually the Japanese found her burning hulk that night and gave her the *coup de grâce*. Kinkaid had decided to withdraw, having no carriers left to oppose the Japanese battleships. So the Battle of Santa Cruz, the last of the great carrier confrontations of 1942, came to a close with another tactical victory for the Japanese. *Zuiho* and *Shokaku* were crippled, but they did not sink, although it was nine months before *Shokaku* was operational again. Against that, *Hornet* was gone and *Enterprise* was damaged. Until she was repaired the Allies had no carriers in the Pacific.

But it was a Pyrrhic victory for the Japanese, who could not afford many more like it. Over a hundred aircraft and their priceless experienced aircrews had been lost. The Americans, on the other hand, could afford losses; new aircraft were beginning to roll off the assembly lines and a great aircrew training programme was gathering way in the United States. But Nagumo's dead airmen were gone for ever.

In November the Japanese High Command decided, belatedly, that one more major effort, one more heave, would take Guadalcanal. In the first ten days of that month the Tokyo Express made sixty-five destroyer and two cruiser troop-carrying runs. By the 12th the Japanese actually outnumbered the Americans on Guadalcanal for the first time. Yamamoto planned a similar effort at sea, to reach a conclusion with Halsey's carriers once and for all. So the scene was set for the naval battle of Guadalcanal, which lasted from the afternoon of 12 November until 1 a.m. on the morning of the 15th. It was one of the biggest sea-fights of the whole war. Had it taken place in the North Sea or in the Western Approaches it would now be as famous as Jutland.

Large American reinforcements, due to unload on 11/12 November, sailed in two parts: three freighters escorted by Scott in *Atlanta* and four destroyers, and four transports escorted by Rear-Admiral Daniel Callaghan in *San Francisco* with the cruisers *Portland*, *Helena*, and *Juneau* and five destroyers. Kinkaid's task force of *Enterprise*, the battleships *South Dakota* and *Washington*, two cruisers and eight destroyers would provide distant cover and a counter to Yamamoto. If *Enterprise*, being repaired at Noumea, could not reach the battle in time, the two battlewagons and four destroyers would be detached to act independently, under Rear-Admiral Lee.

Both reinforcement parties arrived safely, and the action began on the afternoon of the 12th with a Japanese air attack, successfully beaten off, on the transports unloading at Guadalcanal. Aircraft and intelligence reported a very powerful Tokyo Express of two battleships, four cruisers and eight destroyers, heading down the Slot. Kinkaid's ships were too far away to assist. Callaghan would just have to do his best.

Drawing a mistaken lesson from Cape Esperance, Callaghan had his ships in line ahead, with four destroyers ahead, then *Atlanta* with Scott embarked, then *San Francisco* and the three remaining cruisers, with four destroyers bringing up the rear. This was an admirable formation for navigation and for ship-to-ship communication but for battle it was more suitable for sailing-ship tactics. Furthermore, the cruisers with the best radar were not in leading positions and the two destroyers with the most modern sets were actually in the back four. Many of the ships had not exercised together before, but no combat intelligence was passed to them, nor did Callaghan issue specific instructions. By placing four of his destroyers at the rear, and keeping all eight closely under his personal control, Callaghan deprived them of the chance to use their best weapon, independent torpedo attack.

The first radar indication of the Japanese was at 1.24 a.m. on Friday the 13th. At that time Callaghan's ships were steaming westward past Lunga Point on the north coast of Guadalcanal, having seen the transports safely to their destination. The Japanese raiding group, commanded by Rear-Admiral Abe, included the battleships *Hiei* and *Kirishima*, screened by destroyers and the light cruiser *Nagara*. Heading south-east into Ironbottom Sound, leaving Savo close to port, Abe was not expecting battle. His object was to pound Henderson into helplessness. The Japanese still expected the American ships to leave the Slot and go home with the setting sun.

Callaghan did not turn to starboard, to cross his enemy's T, nor did he send his destroyers on ahead. He appeared to aim for a head-on encounter, for he turned his force to starboard, into an oblique crossing approach in front of the Japanese ships. The leading destroyer *Cushing* sighted two Japanese destroyers at close range at 1.41 and had to make an emergency turn to avoid a collision. This threw Callaghan's following ships into some confusion, which soon became complete. Callaghan delayed a fatal eight minutes before giving the order to open fire, and a wild mêlée in the darkness began.

Atlanta was lit up by searchlight, hit by one torpedo and by gunfire on the bridge. She came to a dead stop, and Scott was amongst those killed. *San Francisco* steamed between the Japanese battleships, *Hiei* to port and *Kirishima* to starboard: she was hit several times and Callaghan himself was killed. *Cushing* was sunk by *Hiei* and the destroyer *Laffey* was sunk by a Japanese destroyer. The destroyers' and cruisers' fire set *Hiei* ablaze from end to end and both battleships reversed course. The destroyer *Sterett* torpedoed and sank the Japanese destroyer *Yudichi* but was then torpedoed and put out of action herself. *Portland* took one torpedo astern and could only steam in circles. *Juneau* was also hit but survived until the morning, when she was sunk by the Japanese submarine I.26 as she was trying to retire. The destroyer *Barton* was hit by two torpedoes and broke in two. She was brand new and had been in action only seven minutes. Another destroyer, *Monssen*, was left a burning hulk. Altogether, Callaghan's ships had taken a grim mauling. But Abe cancelled the bombardment of Henderson.

On 13 November torpedo and bomb attacks by aircraft from Henderson, from *Enterprise*, then steaming up from the south, and

An American transport burning
off Guadalcanal

from Espiritu Santo, caught *Hiei* off Savo Island. She turned over
and sank at 6 p.m. That night, the cruisers *Suzuya* and *Maya*,
under Admiral Nishimura, bombarded Henderson for nearly
forty minutes.

Halsey refused to allow *Enterprise* to operate north of
Guadalcanal and as she was still under repair (with workmen still
on board her) he detached the battleships under Lee to go into
Ironbottom Sound and 'clean up'. Approaching Lee's force was
Admiral Kondo, flying his flag in the cruiser *Atago*, with *Kirishima*
and three more cruisers, bent on delivering the bombardment of
Henderson which Callaghan had forestalled the night before.
Lee's ships entered Ironbottom Sound from the north at
10.15 p.m. on the 14th. Unknown to Lee, he had already been
sighted by the light cruiser *Sendai*, who was shadowing him. Lee
opened fire on *Sendai* at 11.17 p.m. whilst his four destroyers had
a private battle with Japanese destroyers close under the shadow
of Savo; the U.S. destroyers had decidedly the worst of it. *Preston*
and *Walke* were sunk, *Gwin* and *Benham* were badly damaged.
South Dakota had a critical power failure at a crucial time, so that
she was unable to fire and became nothing more than a target
herself, but *Washington*, superbly handled and fought, opened
fire by radar on *Kirishima* at a range of 8,400 yards just after
midnight. In a brisk seven minutes of firing she hit *Kirishima* with
nine out of seventy-five 16-inch shells and another forty 5-inch.
Kirishima was battered into a helpless blazing wreck, and was later
scuttled. Kondo retired at twenty-five minutes past midnight and
returned to Rabaul, where Yamamoto relieved him of his com-

mand (as he had already relieved Abe the day before). In one of the very few battleship engagements of the war, *Washington* had held the ring for the Allies at a very important time, for the naval battles of November were the turning point of the campaign. The Japanese Navy now proposed that Guadalcanal be abandoned, but the Army insisted on carrying on.

Rear-Admiral Tanaka—'Tenacious Tanaka'—was one of the ablest admirals of the war on any side. Brave, wily and quick to recover from surprise, he continued to teach the U.S. Navy almost to the end of the Guadalcanal campaign that any mistakes would be harshly punished. Ironically, Tanaka's last major action was against a special group formed because CincPac's staff had decided that their ships and commanders lacked the true offensive spirit. Kinkaid was appointed to command a new striking force, based on Espiritu Santo, of the heavy cruisers *Minneapolis*, *Pensacola*, *New Orleans* and *Northampton*, the light cruiser *Honolulu* and a destroyer escort. But Kinkaid was relieved on 28 November, to take command in the North Pacific. His successor was the unfortunate Rear-Admiral Carleton Wright, who saw action only two days after assuming command, and against the redoubtable Tanaka himself.

It was Tanaka's Tokyo Express again—eight destroyers, six of them with their decks crammed with troops and stores—but a Tokyo Express in somewhat reduced circumstances. This was no massive reinforcement. The destroyers were to dash inshore off Tassafaronga, throw drums of stores overboard, put troops over the side to be picked up by small craft, and retire again. But Tanaka's ships met Wright's force before arriving at Tassafaronga.

Once again, the Americans had the precious advantage of prior radar contact. Once again, the chance was fumbled. One of the leading destroyers, *Fletcher*, with the latest radar, picked up Tanaka's ships at 11.16 p.m., broad on the port beam, heading in towards the Guadalcanal shore. *Fletcher* asked permission to fire torpedoes, but Wright delayed a priceless four minutes before replying. It was then too late. By the time the torpedoes were launched, the Japanese ships had passed on an opposing course and the range was too great. Not one of the American torpedoes hit. When the last had gone, Wright's cruisers opened fire.

Tanaka and his highly trained torpedo tube crews reacted quickly and launched more than twenty Long Lances in a few moments. They were helped by the cruisers' concentration on only one destroyer, *Takanami*. Only five minutes after the action had opened, the Long Lances began to score: two hits on *Minneapolis*, knocking her out of the firing line; one on *New Orleans*, blowing off her bows and fo'c's'le up to No. 2 turret; one on *Pensacola* amidships; and two on *Northampton*. *Honolulu* alone escaped, by adroit seamanship. Excellent damage control saved

Rear-Admiral Raizo 'Tenacious' Tanaka, driver of the Tokyo Express

all but *Northampton*, who sank after a three-hour struggle to save her, but the damaged cruisers were out of the war for nearly a year. Of Tanaka's force, only *Takanami* was sunk. The battle of Tassafaronga, as both sides realized, reflected the greatest credit on the Imperial Japanese Navy: eight destroyers, surprised and with their upper decks cluttered with men and gear, had inflicted great damage on a superior force of cruisers which had been lying in wait for them.

Guadalcanal continued to teach basic lessons of modern sea warfare to the bitter end. On 23 January reconnaissance reported considerable Japanese shipping activity north of the island. This was believed to be another Tokyo Express but in fact was an evacuation force: the Japanese had at last decided to abandon what had become a costly and open-ended commitment. On the 29th Halsey sent up a decoy reinforcement group, covered by cruisers, destroyers and two *Sangamon* Class escort carriers, hoping to lure Yamamoto into action again. This group, under Rear-Admiral Robert Giffen, was off Rennell Island on 29 January when it was attacked at dusk by torpedo-carrying Bettys from the newly constructed airfield at Munda in New Georgia. Giffen's ships were poorly disposed to repel an air attack, his captains had no orders what to do, and, most culpable of all, Giffen had left behind his carriers for some minor reason and had no air cover. Trusting to his anti-aircraft fire, he pressed on, but one torpedo hit *Chicago*, the sole survivor of Savo, and left her dead in the water. Attempts were made to take her in tow but Japanese aircraft found her again at 4 p.m. the next day and, despite air cover from *Enterprise*, sank her with four more torpedoes. This was the seventh and last naval battle of Guadalcanal. The Japanese began to evacuate their troops on 2 February. Their security was magnificent and by the 7th the last Japanese soldier had been spirited away by the Tokyo Express, running in reverse, under the Allies' very noses.

The U.S. Navy had many bloody lessons off Guadalcanal, losing hundreds of men and many valuable ships. But in general they profited from experience and in the end had sunk as many Japanese ships—twenty-five—as they had lost themselves. When Guadalcanal was secured for the Allies, Australian troops had already inflicted on the Japanese their first defeat of the war on land, in Papua, where the Australians had counter-attacked in September 1942, forced the Japanese to retreat along the Kokoda Trail, and by 31 January 1943 had fought their way across the Owen Stanley mountain range and reached Buna, on the north coast of New Guinea. The Australians, in this little known campaign, suffered almost twice the casualties sustained by the U.S. Marines on Guadalcanal, but together the Australians in Papua and the Americans on Henderson had shown that the Japanese were not invincible, not at sea, not in the air, and now not in the jungle either.

6 FORWARD IN THE SOLOMONS

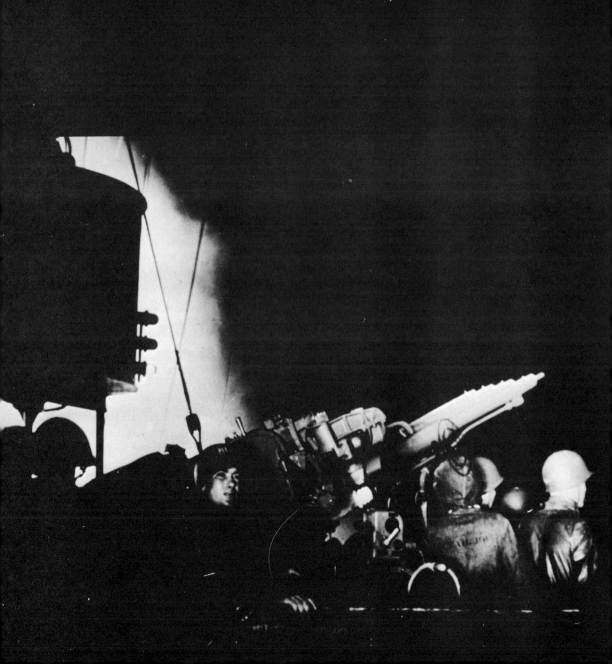

After Guadalcanal, the Allies could win the war in the Pacific,
and win it quickly, provided the right choice of strategies was
made. With the weight of American war production and the sheer
variety of American technological invention, the Allies had the
beating of the Japanese, although in 1943 there was some way to
go, many mistakes to be made and many losses suffered before
victory could be clearly seen. Early in 1943, two naval actions took
place which demonstrated the great range of response required
in the Pacific to defeat the Japanese. The actions were thousands
of miles apart and totally dissimilar: in one no Allied ships took
part, in the other, no aircraft.

Exasperated by their reverses in New Guinea, the Japanese
despatched a whole infantry division of some 7,000 troops from
Rabaul on 1 March, embarked in seven transports and a collier,
escorted by eight destroyers. The convoy passed into the Bismarck
Sea that night and, though bad weather concealed it at first, it
was sighted on the 2nd. Aircraft of the U.S.A.A.F. and R.A.A.F.
from Papua began a series of attacks which lasted intermittently
for thirty-six hours. By 4 March the whole convoy of eight ships
and four of the destroyers had been sunk, for the loss of two Allied
bombers and three fighters. This Battle of the Bismarck Sea was a
smashing victory for air power at sea, one of the greatest of the
war, equivalent to a major engagement on land. It ensured that
the Japanese never again attempted to move anything larger
than a small barge by daylight within range of Allied aircraft.

Later that month, a curiously old-fashioned naval action was
fought off the Komandorski Islands, between Kamchatka and
the Aleutians. It was a gun battle between ships which had
almost a First World War period flavour about it. The Aleutians,
with their foul climate and dreary scenery, were, as both sides
had found out, much better left to the native Aleuts. But as the
Japanese had taken Kiska and Attu, they had to maintain them.
On 26 March 1943 a task group of the light cruiser *Richmond*
(flag), heavy cruiser *Salt Lake City*, and four destroyers under
Rear-Admiral Charles H. McMorris U.S.N. encountered a
superior Japanese force of two heavy cruisers *Maya* and *Nachi*
(flag), two light cruisers and four destroyers, under Vice-Admiral
Hosogaya, escorting a group of transports to the Aleutians. The
two sides met, the Americans to the south, the Japanese to the
north, just after 8 a.m. on a cold clear morning, and began to
exchange salvoes at ranges of between ten and twelve miles.
McMorris tried to work northwards to reach the transports but
the Japanese cut him off, concentrating their fire on *Salt Lake
City*, who scored hits on *Nachi* but was herself hit twice and at one
point came to a stop in the water. With *Salt Lake City* almost
helpless, McMorris had to retire westwards under cover of a
thick smokescreen which the Japanese, having no radar, found
impenetrable. Had Hosagaya penetrated the smokescreen he
would have found *Salt Lake City* easy prey but somewhat timidly

he retired, hotly pursued by three of McMorris's destroyers. Hosogaya was shortly afterwards relieved of his command. Attu was retaken by the U.S. 7th Infantry Division in May 1943, despite a final suicidal 'banzai' charge by a thousand screaming Japanese. Plans were formed to retake Kiska in July but the Japanese evacuated the island. The Aleutians then dropped out of the action picture for the rest of the war.

In the South Pacific the battle shifted northwards into the central Solomons, where the Japanese, though constantly harassed by Allied air attacks, ship bombardments and offensive mine-laying, extended the airfield at Munda, building others at Vila, on Kolombangara Island and in southern Bougainville, and seaplane bases in the Shortlands and other islands. But these were defensive measures, which did not satisfy Yamamoto. In April he launched Operation 'I', which was intended to be a crushing air offensive against Allied shipping and bases in Guadalcanal, Papua and Australia. He disembarked some 170 aircraft from his four fleet carriers to double the existing air strength of the 11th Air Fleet ashore in Rabaul. Huge formations, of between 100 and 200 planes, swept down the Slot on 1 April, attacked Tulagi on the 7th, Oro Bay near Buna on the 11th, Port Moresby on the 12th, and Milne Bay on the 24th.

The Japanese aircrews, understandably, claimed tremendous successes, which Yamamoto believed. In fact, they had sunk the U.S. destroyer *Aaron Ward*, the U.S. tanker *Kanawha*, the Australian minesweeper *Pirie*, the New Zealand anti-submarine trawler *Moa* and a handful of small merchant ships, and damaged several more, for the loss of some dozens of aircraft and their priceless naval aircrews. The offensive was not only a failure in material terms, but a gross strategic error. Instead of flinging his precious aircrews against greatly reinforced Allied land bases, Yamamoto would have done far better to have held them back against the day when they would surely be needed against Halsey's and Spruance's carriers.

Yamamoto himself did not live to know of his failure. On 14 April Allied intelligence at Pearl Harbor decoded signals giving the precise details of a tour of inspection he would shortly be making in the central Solomons. On the 18th the Sally bomber carrying the fleet commander and his staff was ambushed and shot down over southern Bougainville by sixteen Lightning fighters from Henderson Field. None of the passengers or crew survived. So passed the man who had fashioned Japan's early victories. His death was in its way a symbol of Japan's declining fortunes.

This decline was not so evident at the time, however. In 1943 MacArthur's forces in the South-west Pacific advanced upon Rabaul on two fronts, with a sequence of 'leap-frogging' amphibious operations along the north coast of New Guinea and in the Solomons. MacArthur's troops were transported by the Seventh Amphibious Force under Rear-Admiral Daniel Barby (known as 'Uncle Dan, the Amphibious Man') and supported at sea by the Seventh Fleet (so designated in March 1943), commanded first by Admiral Carpender and then by Kinkaid. By December 1943 they had landed at Nassau Bay, Lae and Finschhafen, and Cape Gloucester in New Britain; in the Solomons, New Georgia, Vella Lavella and Bougainville had all been invaded. The campaigns on land were accompanied by another series of sea fights, as at Guadalcanal, and still more attrition of Japanese aircrews. The Japanese lost an estimated 2,500 aircraft attempting to recapture Guadalcanal and in the subsequent defence of the central Solomons. At sea, the actions showed once again that though there was ample scope for the flair and daring of an individual American commander, the Japanese Long Lance torpedo was still the arbiter of naval battle in the Solomons.

After an unopposed landing on the Russell Islands on 30 June 1943, the main landing on New Georgia took place the next day and another bitter campaign began, in tropical jungle conditions similar to Guadalcanal, though not as protracted. Even so the islands were not secured until October, the Japanese reinforcing themselves at every opportunity by another Tokyo Express which once again the Navy had to interrupt as best they could. The first engagement was the Battle of Kula Gulf, on the night of 5/6 July. A support group of the 6-inch gun cruisers *Honolulu* (flag), *Helena* and *St Louis*, with four destroyers, under Rear-Admiral Ainsworth entered Kula Gulf to engage a Japanese Tokyo Express heading for Vila and consisting of two transport groups of three and four destroyers respectively, carrying troops and supplies, escorted by three more destroyers, *Suzukaze, Tanikaze* and *Niizuki* (flying the flag of Rear-Admiral Teruo Akiyama).

All the American ships were fitted with excellent SG surface warning radar, and Ainsworth's cruisers' 6-inch guns, in triple turrets, had a very rapid rate of fire. As in battles off Guadalcanal, technological superiority lay with the American ships, but the disadvantages were compensated by superior Japanese seamanship and training. Akiyama ran down the eastern side of Kolombangara, detached his first transport group of three destroyers and turned back to the north as Ainsworth's ships cleared the north-eastern point of New Georgia. Ainsworth detected Akiyama by radar at 1.40 a.m., range over twelve miles. He turned to port to close the range and then to starboard again, in the standard line-ahead fighting formation, nine minutes later. It was the same unwieldy line, with destroyers disposed ahead and astern, which had been so often used off Guadalcanal.

Akiyama had detached his second transport group for Vila when his lookouts sighted Ainsworth's cruisers against a clear northern horizon. He recalled his transport group. ordered 30 knots, and attacked. Ainsworth meanwhile waited until the range had come down to 6,800 yards before opening fire. When his ships did fire, they concentrated on *Niizuki*, leading. *Niizuki* was soon shattered and left sinking, but the other two destroyers successfully fired their sixteen Long Lances and retired to reload. The American destroyers were still tied ineffectively to their tactical formation.

Three torpedoes hit *Helena*, and she sank in a few minutes, until only a portion of her severed bows, still floating, showed above water; 168 of her people were lost. *Helena* had been a much-loved ship and the feelings of her survivors summed up those of the hundreds of men whose ships were sunk in those waters. 'It was a sad, an unbelievably sad moment. What does one say? Not what you might expect. Nothing smart or slick. Just the so-called corny phrases you have heard time and again in the movies or read in fiction: "She was a grand ship." "She sure was swell." She went down gracefully and quickly, like the queen that she was.'[16]

Sporadic skirmishes and firing went on almost until dawn, as the Japanese continued their runs to Vila and the Americans paused to pick up survivors, and then went into action again. Akiyama was killed, and Ainsworth regarded as a victor, until fuller facts became known later. Rear Admiral 'Tip' Merrill, also commanding a task force, signalled Ainsworth: 'I am afraid you have spoiled the hunting by taking too much game on your last hunt.'

Merrill was mistaken, as was quickly demonstrated when Ainsworth's ships were in action again in the Battle of Kolombangara on the night of 12/13 July. Another Tokyo Express, of four destroyer-transports escorted by the destroyers *Mikazuki*, *Yukikaze*, *Hamakaze*, *Kiyonami* and *Yugure*, led by Rear-Admiral Shunji Izaki in Tanaka's old flagship *Jintsu*, left Rabaul for Vila at 5 a.m. on the 12th. Ainsworth flew his flag in *Honolulu*, with *St Louis* and the light cruiser H.M.N.Z.S. *Leander*, slower, more lightly armed and with a larger turning circle than the U.S. cruisers. He also had nine destroyers, in two squadrons.

A Catalina sighted Izaki's force shortly after midnight, north of Vella Lavella, and heading south-east at 30 knots for Kula Gulf. Ainsworth formed his ships in single line ahead, five destroyers ahead of the cruisers and four astern. The line was six miles long, steering west at 26 knots. However, Ainsworth was ready to let his destroyers go at an early stage in the action.

Jintsu was fitted with a new electronic device which detected radar transmissions at twice the range of radar detection. Using this, Izaki had a good idea of his enemy's position and track. Despatching his four transports to unload on Kolombangara he advanced towards Ainsworth's ships. He was anxious to close the critical gap between the range at which Ainsworth's radar would detect him and the range at which he could fire his Long Lances. Ainsworth was just as anxious to close, having decided to open fire when the range was between eight and ten thousand yards,

'General quarters!' Five-inch gun crew on board a U.S. carrier

and being still ignorant of the Long Lance. Both sides approached at a combined speed of 58 knots.

At 1.12 a.m., when the range had come down to 10,000 yards, Ainsworth turned his ships to port to bring all guns to bear, and opened fire. *Jintsu*, like *Niizuki* before her, took the brunt of the fire and was thumped to a dead stop. After his rear destroyers had fired torpedoes, one of which hit the stationary *Jintsu*, Ainsworth turned his ships through 180°. But the Long Lances were on their way. *Leander*, less quick to turn, and suffering a TBS fade-away at a crucial moment, was knocked out of the battle and had to limp away to Tulagi.

Mikazuki was separated from the other destroyers and took no more part. The remaining four, however, retired to reload and half an hour later they were back. There was some doubt about whether they were Japanese or American. Ainsworth's ships steered steady courses, making perfect torpedo targets, while they made up their minds. *Honolulu*, *St Louis* and the destroyer *Gwin* were all hit. The two cruisers followed *Leander* back to Tulagi, but *Gwin* went down. Once again, the Japanese had shown their truly superb night-fighting skill. Happily for the Allies, the true results of these encounters were not known for some time, and in fact Kolombangara was yet another Japanese Pyrrhic victory. The Japanese Navy kept on winning these undoubted tactical victories, but every one left them with fewer ships, unable to replace their losses.

Success or failure in these night encounters in the Solomons ultimately depended on the quality of the men involved. This was clearly demonstrated in one undoubted victory for the U.S. Navy in the Vella Gulf, west of Kolombangara, on the night of 6/7 August. Another Tokyo Express was reported to be on its way. The Allies had no cruisers available (partly due to the depredations of previous actions) so six destroyers, under Commander F. Moosbrugger U.S.N., were dispatched to do what they could. By 10.30 Moosbrugger's ships were steaming up the west coast of Kolombangara at 25 knots in two divisions of line ahead, the second division of three destroyers in station some 60° abaft Moosbrugger's starboard beam.

The Japanese force consisted of four destroyers, *Hagikaze*, *Arashi* and *Kawakaze* carrying troops and supplies, with the flotilla commander Captain Sigiura in *Shigure*. For once the Japanese were unusually unwary and failed to see Moosbrugger's ships, masked by the blackness of Kolombangara Island. Their first inkling of danger was the sight of the white water boiling under the sterns of the American destroyers as they turned away, having fired torpedoes at 4,000 yards. *Hagikaze*, *Arashi* and *Kawakaze* were all hit by torpedoes, or subsequent gunfire, or both, and sank, two of them blowing up with such a violent flash and detonation that men thirty miles away thought it was the volcano on Kolombangara erupting. Only *Shigure* escaped,

The campaign in New Guinea

Above: A Papuan infantryman at Bren gun drill
Right: An Australian machine-gun section on patrol in the jungle
Below: Australian and American soldiers inspect knocked out
Japanese tanks

Below: A Japanese Zero fighter burning at Lae after a raid by Allied planes

Bottom: An American gun crew engaging an isolated Japanese machine-gun post

Opposite above: Dawn, 15
August 1943. American assault
troops heading for the beach at
Vella Lavella in the Solomons

Opposite below: American
assault troops off Vella Lavella

Sigiura deciding that discretion was the better part of valour.
Moosbrugger took his own ships away triumphantly untouched,
after one of the neatest and quickest tactical victories of the war.

The island of Vella Lavella was invaded on 15 August and by
1 October the last remaining 600 Japanese troops on the island
were pinned on the north-west shore. The Japanese operation to
evacuate these troops led to the battle of Vella Lavella on the
night of 6/7 October. The Japanese had nine destroyers and a
dozen small craft under Rear-Admiral Ijuin, the Allies six
destroyers under Captain Frank R. Walker U.S.N. It was another
'shoot-out' between destroyers and Walker was fastest on the
draw, firing torpedoes first at 7,000 yards and sinking *Yugumo*.
But Long Lances sank *Chevalier* and Walker's own *Selfridge*, while
O'Bannon was badly damaged by collision. Meanwhile Ijuin's
small craft successfully took off the troops. With their soldiers
safely away, and two destroyers for one, the tactical balance
went again to the Japanese. But *Yugumo* was the fortieth of their
destroyers lost since the war began, and Japanese shipyards were
simply not making good that rate of loss.

The next step towards Rabaul was Bougainville. After heavy
air raids to damp down Japanese activity at Rabaul, U.S. Marines
and New Zealand troops landed at Cape Torokina, Empress
Augusta Bay, on 1 November 1943. That night the Japanese, as
expected, attempted another counter-coup such as they had
achieved off Savo Island in August. But this was not to be another
Savo. The U.S. Navy had come a long way and a hard way since
that terrible night. The lives and ships lost, then and since, had
not been lost in vain. Ships' routines had been changed to
mitigate combat fatigue in the crews. Radar presentation and
interpretation, ship-to-air radio liaison, TBS voice discipline and
combat information centres had all been improved. Above all
some idea of the deadliness of the Long Lance torpedo had at last
been realized and the force commander Rear-Admiral Aaron S.
Merrill, although he would still go into battle in single line ahead,
gave his destroyer captains greater independence much
earlier in the action. He also intended to manoeuvre his enemy up
to twenty miles from the transport anchorages, to stand off and
engage at ranges of nineteen to twenty thousand yards, and, most
important, avoid steaming on steady courses. By the time the
Long Lances reached where he should have been, he would be
long gone.

Merrill flew his flag in the cruiser *Montpelier*, with the new
6-inch gun cruisers *Cleveland*, *Columbia* and *Denver*. Ahead, he had
Captain Arleigh ('Thirty-One-Knot') Burke's Division 45, of
four destroyers, and astern, Commander B. L. Austin's Division
46, also of four destroyers. His task was to place his ships 'across the
entrance to Empress Augusta Bay and to prevent the entry
therein of a single enemy ship', and as night fell on 1 November,
Merrill steered north so to do.

A U.S. cruiser bombarding
Buka airfield off the northern
tip of Bougainville by night

His opponent was Rear-Admiral Sentaro Omori, with the two heavy cruisers *Myoko* (flag) and *Haguro*, screened to port by the light cruiser *Sendai* and three destroyers, to starboard by the light cruiser *Agano* and three destroyers. Omori had started out with five destroyer-transports for a counter-landing, but finding that they could do no more than 26 knots and determined to succeed himself where Mikawa had failed, he had sent the transports back to Rabaul and came on southwards himself at 32 knots.

When *Montpelier's* first radar contact was obtained at 2.30 a.m. on 2 November, range just over eighteen miles, Burke's van destroyers altered towards at once to attack the nearest Japanese column, led by *Sendai*. Merrill then reversed his cruisers' course so that Austin's destroyers now became the van, intending them to attack in turn. But his ships were illuminated by a Japanese aircraft flare, and were seen from *Sendai*. Omori turned his ships to starboard to close, frustrating Burke's torpedo attack. Merrill

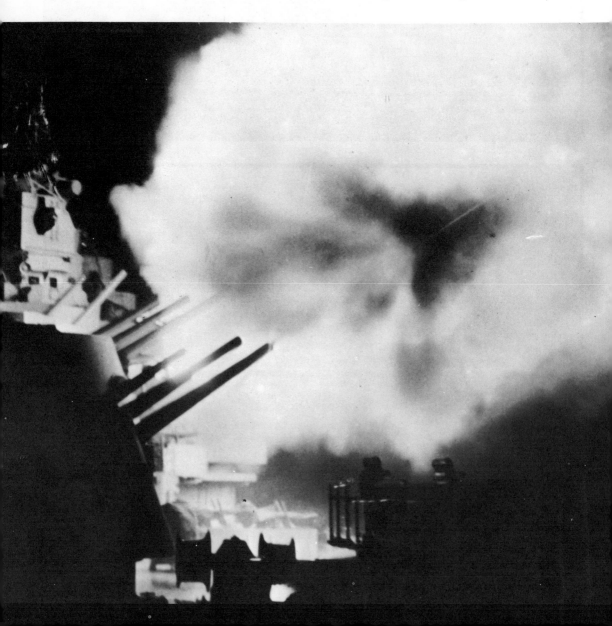

could wait no longer and opened fire. Radar controlled fire tended to concentrate upon one target and the focus this time was *Sendai*, who was quickly hit several times and forced out of the action. While Burke's twenty-five torpedoes were missing, Merrill altered course outwards, to keep his stand-off range, while his cruisers made smoke to counteract the brilliant Japanese flares. Maintaining a range of 19,000 yards, Merrill's cruisers shifted aim to the Japanese cruisers and hit *Haguro*. *Denver* was hit in return. Shortly after 3 a.m. Merrill led his ships through an elaborate sequence of course changes, stepping and side-stepping, turning and weaving, to avoid giving a target for the Long Lances. His cruiser captains followed him with admirable skill, despite the smoke and din of the battle.

Omori had always over-estimated the forces against him and when he thought he had sunk two enemy cruisers he broke off the battle at 3.37 a.m. and ordered a general retirement. The U.S. destroyers regrouped, but had mixed fortunes. Austin, in particular, was fired on by his own side, lost *Foote* who was torpedoed and had to be towed in next day, collided in his own ship *Spence* with *Thatcher*, was hit once and holed by a friendly shell, came under fire from Burke, missed a perfect chance of a torpedo attack as Japanese ships passed close to on a reciprocal course, exchanged shots with two retiring Japanese destroyers. Burke's Division 45 came upon and gave the *coup de grâce* to *Sendai* and later dispatched the crippled destroyer *Hatsukaze*. Merrill recalled his destroyers at first light.

In two and a half days of bombardment, surface and anti-aircraft action, Merrill's cruisers expended 27,000 rounds of ammunition of various calibres, while his destroyers fired fifty-two torpedoes, for *Sendai*, *Hatsukaze*, damage to *Myoko* and *Haguro*, and some slight damage to *Agano*. Yet it was certainly a victory, for which 'Tip' Merrill well deserved the kudos he received, whilst Omori was relieved of his command.

On 5 November Vice-Admiral Kurita led a force of six heavy cruisers to repair Omori's omission, but aircraft from *Saratoga* and *Princeton*, flown off some 200 miles south-east of Rabaul, attacked and damaged five of the cruisers, forcing Kurita to retire to Truk. This was a decisive tilt in the balance of power. Command of the sea round the Solomons now passed to the Allies. On the 11th, a carrier task group of *Essex*, *Bunker Hill* and the light carrier *Independence*, escorted by ten destroyers, under Rear-Admiral Alfred E. Montgomery, struck at shipping in Rabaul, damaging a light cruiser and two destroyers with torpedoes. The Japanese retaliated with a massive strike of sixty-seven Zekes, twenty-seven Vals and fourteen Kates which seemed to fill the sky, so that one fighter pilot was heard to say 'Jesus Christ! There are millions of them! Let's go to work.' They went to work and shot down thirty-two Zekes, twenty-four Vals and twelve Kates, in exchange for a few bomb near misses on the carriers. Thus, only slight

damage was inflicted on Japanese shipping, but great slaughter wrought amongst Japanese aircraft. Admiral Koga, who had replaced Yamamoto, withdrew naval aircrews from Rabaul the next day. A little more of Japanese air strength had been bled away, just at the time when the 'Atoll War' was beginning in the central Pacific.

On 24 November the Japanese attempted to reinforce Buka Island, north of New Georgia, with another Tokyo Express. Captain Arleigh Burke, whose destroyers were refuelling that day, received a characteristically crisply worded signal from Halsey: 'Thirty-One-Knot Burke, get this. Put your squadron athwart the Buka-Rabaul evacuation line about thirty-five miles west of Buka. If no enemy contacts by early morning, come south to refuel same place. If enemy contacted you know what to do, HALSEY.'

Burke certainly did know what to do. To assist him, he had his own Division 45 with *Charles Ausburne, Claxton* and *Dyson*, and Austin's Division 46, with *Spence* and *Converse*. His adversary was Captain Kiyoto Kagawa, with the destroyers *Onami* and *Makinami*, screening Captain Katsumori Yamashiro's three destroyer-transports *Amagiri, Yuguri* and *Uzuki*, which were to land 900 troops on Buka and evacuate 700 useless personnel. Burke placed his ships in two divisions, 5,000 yards apart, to the western end of his search area, guessing this would give a better chance of interception, and he was rewarded at 1.41 a.m. on 25 November by three radar contacts, eleven miles to the eastward. It was Kagawa's screen, returning from their mission.

Burke led his division towards the enemy and attacked with fifteen torpedoes at 1.56 a.m., range 6,000 yards, torpedo running range 4,500. The Japanese lookouts were slow and Kagawa had little time to evade. *Onami* disintegrated in a ball of flame 300 feet high. *Makinami's* back was broken. *Charles Ausburne* now had another radar contact: Yamashiro's three transports, 13,000 yards behind Kagawa. Telling Austin to finish off *Makinami*, Burke went after his new quarry. But Yamashiro was equally anxious to get away and Burke had to settle for a long chase, first north and then east, at 33 knots. He opened fire on the rear transport when it came in range. Eventually, some sixty miles east of Cape St George, the most southerly point of New Ireland, Burke had put so many shells into *Yuguri* that she slowed down and gunfire from all three of Burke's ships sunk her. Burke still chased westwards but at 4 a.m., when he was only thirty-three miles off Cape St George, he had to break off, lest dawn catch him close to an enemy coast. Telling Austin, who had meanwhile dispatched *Makinami*, to join him, Burke retired to the east.

Three Japanese destroyers had been sunk, without a single Allied casualty. No Allied ship had even been hit. This Battle of Cape St George was 'an almost perfect action'. It took place on Thanksgiving Day and Burke and his crews duly gave heartfelt thanks for their victory on their return.

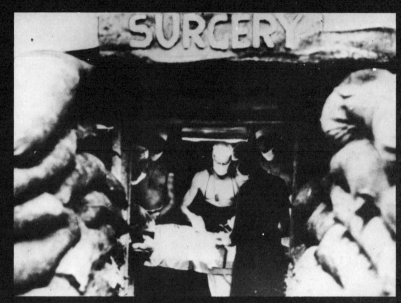

The battle for Bougainville

Above: Try it with chopsticks—
a U.S. Marine captain on
Bougainville Island
Above right: An underground
operating theatre protected
from everything except a direct
hit, Bougainville Island
Right: An American infantryman
about to throw a hand grenade
at a Japanese pillbox
Opposite above: An American
tank giving cover for advancing
infantrymen of the 37th Division
on Bougainville
Opposite below: The other
enemy, the climate—knee-deep
mud on Bougainville Island
after torrential rain

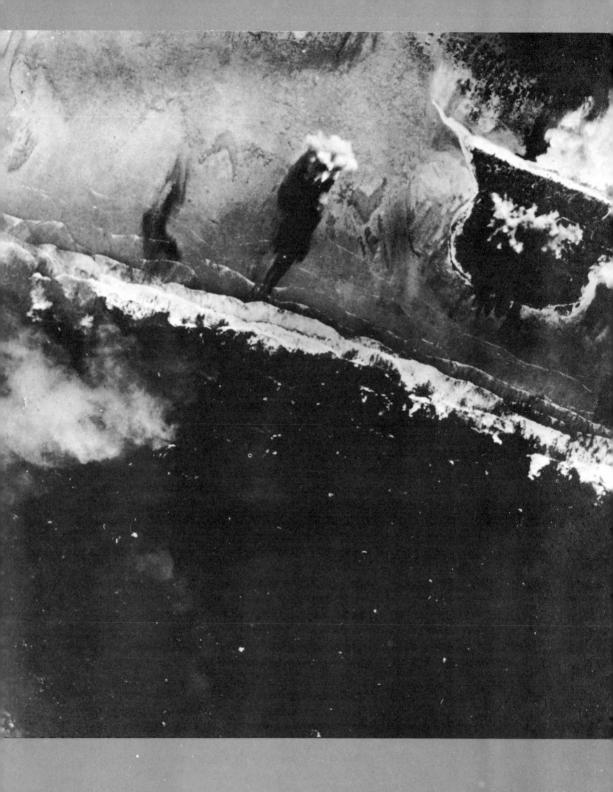

7 THE 'ATOLL WAR'

A bombing raid in progress on Maloelap Atoll in the Marshall Islands

'Last week', wrote *Time* magazine in November 1943, 'some two to three thousand U.S. Marines, most of them now dead or wounded, gave the nation a name to stand beside those of Concord Bridge, the *Bonhomme Richard*, the Alamo, Little Big Horn, and Belleau Wood. The name was Tarawa.' The planning had been done, the decisions made. The ships and aircraft had been built, the men armed and trained. The waiting was over and the great Allied drive across the Central Pacific, from fortified island to fortified island in what became known as the 'Atoll War', had begun with an assault on a hitherto totally unknown atoll in the Gilbert Islands. There at Tarawa, as on Guadalcanal, there were some hard and bloody lessons to be learned.

The advance across the Central Pacific was, in fact, a modified version of the original pre-war American strategy for the Far East. Its objective had been to establish a base at or near Hong Kong from which an invasion of Japan could be launched. An actual invasion of Japan was always implicit in the strategy, although Allied planners also hoped that Japan could be reduced to defeat by bombing, mining and blockade. The Central Pacific strategy became known as the 'Navy plan' and its chief advocates were Admiral Nimitz and his staff. It was also favoured by Admirals King and Leahy on the Joint Chiefs of Staff Committee. The plan had many advantages. It was the shortest route to Japan. It would provide bases for very long-range bombing of the Japanese mainland at an early stage. It would avoid a series of protracted land campaigns under very difficult geographical and climatic conditions. The suicidal resistance of Japanese garrisons had already shown just how protracted such campaigns were bound to be. Above all, the 'Navy plan' would make the fullest use of sea power, the department of war in which the Allies in the Pacific grew stronger with every passing month.

The other continuing advance, in the South-west Pacific, became known as the 'Army plan'. Its chief protagonist was General MacArthur. He had promised the peoples of the Philippines that he would return. He felt that the United States were morally bound to liberate the Philippines at the first opportunity. To Douglas MacArthur, an assault upon metropolitan Japan which left the Philippines still occupied by the Japanese would be unthinkable.

It was most unfortunate that the two strategic advances should have become so closely associated with the 'Army' and 'Navy'. It was true that not all General MacArthur's staff shared his emotional preoccupation with the Philippines, nor were all the naval staff in Washington and Pearl Harbor in total agreement with the 'Navy plan'. But in general the main combatants fell into these two categories, and thus the controversy aroused all the worst aspects of the traditional rivalry between the U.S. Army and the U.S. Navy. It was a saying of Navy men that their chief opponents in this war, in order of priority, were 'first MacArthur,

Essex-class aircraft carrier with Hellcat fighters and Helldiver dive-bombers ranged on the flight deck

then the U.S. Army, and then the Japanese'. It was sometimes hard for outsiders to believe that these two great commands were not, in fact, engaged in fighting each other instead of the Japanese; to go from one to the other was like passing from one autonomous feudal kingdom to another, penetrating frontiers bristling with mutual antipathy and suspicion. The situation could have been remedied, once and for all, by the appointment of a Supreme Allied Commander for the whole of the Pacific. This concept was considered, but never established, because of the vastness of the areas involved and General MacArthur's special position.

For much of 1943 there had been a comparative lull in the Central Pacific. The theatre had been awaiting the arrival of its queen, the *Essex* class aircraft carrier. These magnificent new 27,000-ton, 32-knot vessels were heavily armed with anti-aircraft guns but were designed primarily for attack; they were lightly armoured, but carried an impressive complement of 90 and later 100 aircraft. The first of them arrived at Pearl Harbor on 30 May 1943. By the autumn the Central Pacific Fleet had six heavy carriers including a new *Yorktown* and a new *Lexington*, five new 11,000-ton *Independence* class light carriers, twelve battleships and a host of cruisers, destroyers and landing craft of various types and sizes.

The Japanese had used carriers in their first attack and it was justice that carriers should roll the war back to them. With their deployment of carriers in the Pacific, the U.S. Navy used in a new way some old principles of naval warfare: mobility, surprise, and the concentration of the necessary force at the required point. The fleet, designated the Fifth Fleet and formed on 15 March 1943 out of the Central Pacific component of the Pacific Fleet, was commanded by Raymond Spruance, promoted Vice-Admiral. It was at once the largest, most powerful, flexible and self-sufficient weapon ever forged in naval history. Its spearhead was the Fast Carrier Task Force, designated Task Force 58, commanded by Rear-Admiral Charles Pownall and later by Rear-Admiral Marc A. Mitscher. The task force was organized in separate task groups, each under its own admiral, and each normally containing two heavy and two light carriers, with its own escort of fast battleships, cruisers and destroyers. Task groups could operate independently or in company as a task force. By detaching individual groups to refuel and rearm, the task force as a whole could exert constant pressure on the enemy. In his memoirs after the war, MacArthur complained that his fleet in the South-west Pacific had to make do with 'little carriers'. But there is no doubt that the Chiefs of Staff allocated the big carriers to the big battle. The Fifth Fleet combined extraordinary mobility with fearsome hitting power, and was able to strike at one target and then vanish into the distances of the Pacific, using the very size of the ocean as a defence, before reappearing to strike at another target, hundreds of miles away, a short time later. This unusual degree of flexibility enabled the carriers to give MacArthur the air support he needed at important moments.

During the Allied advance across the Pacific, TF 58's task was to carry out pre-invasion strikes on the target atoll's defences, to give tactical air support to the troops on or approaching the beaches during the assault phase, to maintain air cover while the target atoll was secured and airstrips set up ashore, to strike at distant Japanese island bases to prevent them flying in reinforcements, and to intercept any Japanese attempt by sea or air to attack the troops on the target atoll.

Whilst the carriers and battleships held the distant ring, the Marine and Army assault troops—the Fifth Amphibious Corps, under Major-General Holland M. ('Howling Mad') Smith U.S.M.C.—were carried to the target beaches by Rear-Admiral Richmond Kelly Turner's Fifth Amphibious Force, which was a further large fleet of transports, cargo ships and landing ships and craft, with its own escort of carriers, battleships, cruisers and destroyers. The Fifth Fleet also had its own shore-based air force, under Rear-Admiral John Hoover.

Once the Fifth Fleet had left Pearl Harbor it never returned, as a fleet, until after the war was over. Ships and men were replaced as necessary *in situ*. The fleet used no permanent shore bases. A mobile service force of tankers, repair ships, tenders, ammunition ships and floating docks set up floating bases in lagoons some distance to the rear of operations. These bases were magnificent examples of the American 'can do' spirit. Nothing was impossible, nothing too much trouble for them; ships wearied in combat could return to have damage repaired, personnel replaced, paperwork brought up to date. In the Central Pacific, there could be no question of 'living off the land'. The targets were almost all tiny coral atolls which held nothing of any assistance to the invading force. There was no room for retreats, or holding operations, or perimeter defences, as in Guadalcanal or Bougainville; it was victory, or withdrawal within a few days. Thus ammunition loads had to be nicely calculated and exactly stowed. Food had to be provided for the native populations, who were not well treated by the Japanese, as well as for the combat troops. Every item had to be taken to the scene of action, thousands of miles from Pearl Harbor and even further from the United States. A tanker or a store ship could not make more than two or perhaps three return trips a year to the States. So, to the old art of naval warfare, the Fifth Fleet added the equally old science of logistics, but on a new and global scale.

The first target in the 'Atoll War' was to have been the Marshall Islands, mandated to Japan in 1920 and closed to foreigners for years before the war. But Nimitz decided that the Gilberts must be attacked first, because of their threatening geographical position on the flank of any advance towards the Marshalls. Air photo-reconnaissance showed that the Gilberts were formidably defended. This was very largely the Allies' own fault. The Japanese had taken the Gilberts in December 1941 but had only token forces there until August 1942, when Colonel Carlson's Marine Raiders arrived by submarine for a 'hit-and-run' raid on Butaritari Island, in Makin Atoll. The Japanese then reinforced the atolls, built an airfield on Betio Island in Tarawa Atoll, and began to construct gun emplacements and defences. By the time it was assaulted, Tarawa was garrisoned by 4,500 troops and defended by fourteen guns ranging from 5.5-inch to 8-inch and batteries of field guns ensconced in pillboxes strengthened with logs and armour plate. The troops also had bomb-proof shelters, and the beaches were obstructed by wire and log barricades.

D-Day for Operation GALVANIC, the assault on the Gilbert Islands, was 20 November 1943, five days later than originally planned, but the fact that it took place at all on that date was a miracle of determination and planning by 'Howling Mad' Smith and his staff. Some 200 ships took part, together with 108,000 men, including 27,600 assault and 6,000 garrison troops, with 6,000 vehicles and 117,000 tons of cargo. The first elements of the Northern Attack Force, under Turner, taking one regiment of the 27th U.S. Army Division to Makin, began to sail from Pearl on 21 October. The Northern Attack Force, under Rear-Admiral Harry W. Hill, taking the 2nd Marine Division to Betio, sailed from New Zealand and Efate, beginning on 12 November.

Preliminary air bombing of the targets began next day, 13 November. The fast carriers had begun 'warm-up' strikes on Marcus and Wake islands as well as the target atolls on 1 September. After a pause for recuperation, the carriers returned, deployed in four groups, for a programme of heavy strikes on Tarawa, Makin, Rabaul, Nauru and Jaluit in the Marshalls, between 11 November and D-Day. The bombing raids actually did little damage to the islands' defences but they did cause the garrisons to fire off much of their ammunition, which they had not replaced by D-Day.

D-Day air strikes at Betio began just after dawn (later than planned and required) and were followed by two and a half hours of naval bombardment by three battleships, four cruisers and several destroyers which pounded the island with more than 3,000 tons of high explosive shells. All this greatly encouraged the Marines, waiting to disembark. Physically hard, superbly trained, all veterans of Guadalcanal, the 2nd Marine Division was probably the best military formation in the U.S. armed forces at that time; although they had unshakeable confidence in themselves, the Marines devoutly hoped that all the Japs on that island were now dazed or dead.

However, more Japanese survived the bombardments than was believed humanly possible. There were crucial lapses in radio communications, and gaps in the bombardments allowed the Japanese precious minutes to move their troops into position. There was unexpectedly heavy and alarmingly accurate gunfire from the beaches. The landing craft and amphibious tractors could not all get ashore quickly enough, because an unforeseen low tide stranded them on the coral shelf. Marines had to wade the last hundred yards, thigh deep, under withering fire. Many died in the water and many more were killed as they stepped on the sand. Whole platoons were pinned down, wherever they could

U.S. Marines storming Tarawa

One beautiful smoke-ring—a U.S. cruiser bombarding the assault beaches during the 'Atoll War'

find any cover, for hours. Suddenly, as *Time* reporter Robert Sherrod wrote, 'for the first time I felt that something was wrong. The first waves were not hitting the beach as they should. There were very few boats on the beach, and these were all amphibious tractors that the first wave used. "Oh God, I'm scared," said the little Marine, a telephone operator, who sat next to me forward in the boat. I gritted my teeth and tried to force a smile that would not come and tried to stop quivering all over (now I was shaking from fear). I said, in an effort to be reassuring, "I'm scared too." I never made a more truthful statement in all my life.'[17]

One Marine private, N. M. Baird, an Oneida Indian, was in an amphtrac thirty yards offshore when it was hit. 'The concussion felt like a big fist—Joe Louis maybe—had smacked me right in the face. Seemed to make my face swell up. Knocked me down and sort of stunned me for a moment. I shook my head. Shrapnel was pinging all around. Nicked hell out of my hands and face. One piece about an inch long tore into my back. A fella later pulled it out on shore ... Only about a dozen out of the twenty-five went over the side with me, and only about four of us ever got evacuated.'[18]

U.S. infantry going ashore at Butaritari on Màkin Island

Above : After the first assault : a jetty full of supplies at Tarawa

Opposite : Desolation—Betio Island after the battle

The ordeal of Baird's unit was standard. It took the Marines three days to secure an island which was 2,000 yards long and 500 wide at its broadest point. The last island, Lone Tree, to the north was not taken until the 28th. Casualties among the Navy and Marines engaged amounted to 3,110 killed or wounded. Of the defenders, who had been ordered to fight to the last man, one officer, sixteen men and 129 Korean labourers survived.

At Makin, a hundred miles to the north, the 27th Division took Butaritari in three days, with only 64 killed and 150 wounded. However, at dawn on 24 November the Japanese submarine I.175 torpedoed the escort carrier *Liscome Bay*. The explosion detonated the bombs in a bomb store and the ship was torn apart, sinking in twenty-three minutes, with the loss of 53 officers and 591 of her ship's company.

Despite the losses, which caused great alarm in the American press, Tarawa was an invaluable testing ground, doing for the Allies in the East what Dieppe had done in the West. Bombardment patterns, landing craft designs, disembarkation procedures, ground-to-air radio liaison, rescue of aircrew by submarines, protection of bomb stowages in escort carriers, clothing for combat personnel, methods of assaulting armed strong-points, and scores

of other techniques, routines, designs and plans, were all improved as a result of experience in the Gilberts. Every bit of that experience would be needed for the next assault—against Kwajalein in the Marshall Islands.

Kwajalein was Tarawa writ large—except in American casualties. The largest coral atoll in the world, Kwajalein was even more strongly and formidably defended than Tarawa; indeed it is very probable that without the invaluable experience and indispensable bases the Gilberts provided, the Marshalls invasion would have failed. The majority of the Japanese garrison of some 8,700 men were about equally divided between the main air bases on the adjacent islands of Roi and Namur, in the north-eastern corner, and the main naval base on the largest island of Kwajalein in the south. They were entrenched in massive steel pillboxes and bunkers and were as determined to resist to the last man as those at Tarawa.

For the Allies, some 300 ships took part, not counting the carrier task groups or the submarines, to escort or carry 54,000 assault troops. The Northern Attack Force, under Rear-Admiral Dick Conolly, conveyed the 4th U.S. Marine Division to assault Roi-Namur. The Southern Attack Force, under Turner, took the 7th U.S. Army Division to Kwajalein. A third force in reserve eventually went on to take Eniwetok. D-Day was 31 January, by which time the fast carrier raids had removed the last Japanese air opposition. The whole operation took place with no Japanese air intervention of any kind. The undefended Majuro, abandoned by the Japanese in November 1942, was soon occupied on D-Day and its superb lagoon quickly became a base for the ships of the mobile service squadron. At Roi-Namur, the Marines went ashore in their improved amphtracs and landing craft after a naval bombardment lasting three days which was so heavy and prolonged and delivered from such close range that the grateful Marines dubbed their admiral 'Close-In' Conolly. Once ashore, the Marines cleaned up Roi and Namur and neighbouring islands in a brisk operation lasting just over twenty-six hours.

At Kwajalein, after an equally heavy bombardment (of some 6,000 tons of shells) the 7th Infantry worked methodically through the island from the east and round up to the north, captured it on the 4th and mopped up the final remains on the 5th. Total casualties for the landings were 372 killed and about 1,500 wounded. Of the Japanese, only 100, and 165 Korean labourers, survived. Everybody was well pleased with themselves after Kwajalein. The co-operation between Navy, Army and Marines had been unusually good. Admiral King, never over-lavish with bouquets of praise, sent a signal 'To all hands concerned with the Marshalls operation: Well and smartly done. Carry on.'

The next step was Eniwetok, just over 300 miles west-north-west of Roi-Namur, and only 670 miles from Truk, the great

A well-earned rest at Kwajalein

Japanese stronghold in the Carolines. Known by such names as 'the Gibraltar of the Pacific', Truk was in fact not as strongly defended as legend had it, but it was the best fleet anchorage anywhere in the Japanese mandated islands and had been the regular base for the Combined Fleet since July 1942. Truk's geographical lay-out, of scattered volcanic islands inside a triangular-shaped coral reef, made it impregnable to surface attack from outside its perimeter. But it was open to the air, and a powerful task force including six fleet and four light carriers in three groups under Mitscher (who had relieved Pownall in January) made a fast and undetected run towards Truk in the night of 16/17 February 1944. Spruance himself was present, flying his flag in the battleship *New Jersey* (the fleet commander had also been present during the Marshalls landings, ready to take over command if the Combined Fleet sallied out).

Photo-reconnaissance of Truk on 4 February had shown plenty of targets, but the same reconnaissance had given the game away to Koga, who sent most of his warships to Palau and went back to Japan himself in the giant battleship *Musashi*. But the first of Mitscher's strikes flown off from a point ninety miles north of Truk at dawn on 17 February, of seventy-two fighters followed by eighteen Avengers with incendiaries, found some fifty merchant ships in the harbour and 365 aircraft ranged on the airfields. The strike put all but a hundred of the aircraft out of action. The carriers then mounted more or less continuous strikes of fighters, bombers and torpedo-bombers to work over the airstrips and attack shipping. That evening the Japanese made their only reply, a torpedo attack by Kates who scored a hit on the carrier *Intrepid* (a somewhat unlucky ship, nicknamed 'The Evil I'), putting her out of action for some months.

In the meantime, Spruance in *New Jersey*, with another battleship, *Iowa*, two heavy cruisers and four destroyers, with the light

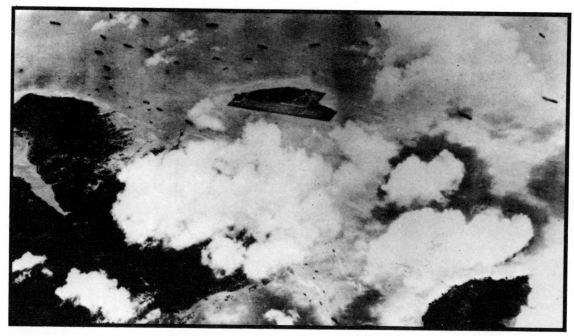

carrier *Cowpens* to give air cover, made one anti-clockwise sweep round Truk to catch any would-be escapers. They sank the light cruiser *Katori* and the destroyer *Maikaze*. That night, a strike of Avengers, specially equipped and trained for night bombing, attacked shipping in the lagoon. It was the first time such a raid had been made in the war and it was a signal success: one-third of the total tonnage destroyed at Truk was sunk by these Avengers. Strikes were resumed again next day, 18 February. Everything that moved had now been sunk or strafed and the aircraft turned their attention to fixed fittings—such as hangars, storage dumps and buildings. When Mitscher's carriers retired at noon, their

Above: The Gibraltar of the Pacific—Truk Lagoon seen from the air, February 1944

Below: Two Japanese ships under attack by U.S. carrier aircraft in Truk Lagoon, 16 February 1944

Right : U.S. Marines just after getting ashore on Eniwetok Atoll

Below : Marines on Eniwetok beach in action against a Japanese pillbox a few hundred yards away

Left: A guard of honour firing a last salute over the burial ground of men who died in the battle for Kwajalein

Below: Seabees building a road on Kwajalein with battleships and other ships in the anchorage

aircraft had flown 1,250 sorties, dropped 400 tons of bombs and torpedoes on shipping and 94 tons of bombs on airfields and shore installations. They had sunk the auxiliary cruisers *Aikoku Maru* and *Kiyosumi Maru,* the destroyers *Fumizuki* and *Oite,* two submarine tenders, an aircraft ferry, six tankers and seventeen other ships—a total loss of about 200,000 tons. This was a crushing blow to the Japanese. Truk was never the same again. The Eniwetok landings were carried out with no air interference at all, and even Allied pilots as far away as Rabaul suddenly noticed the lessening of Japanese air opposition against them.

The capture of Eniwetok Atoll began with landings by the 22nd Marine Regiment on the northerly island of Engebi on 17 February, after the 1,000 defenders had been pounded by a massive air and sea bombardment. The island was taken next day, in a simple invasion, inexpensive of lives. On the two neighbouring southerly islands of Parry and Eniwetok, however, matters went awry. The Japanese had concealed themselves so well that it was believed that the two islands were unoccupied. At the last moment, intelligence material found on Engebi revealed the truth. It was too late to mount a proper bombardment on Eniwetok and the assault troops of the 106th Infantry Regiment, slower, more cautious than the Marines and less well led, made heavy weather of their advance and the island was not taken until the 21st. Parry was bombarded for three days; then the Marines landed on the 22nd and took the island in a day. Of the 3,500 men in the Japanese garrison on Eniwetok Atoll, there were 64 survivors. The Marines got no elation from their bloody victory. One of them, Lieutenant Cord Meyer, wrote later, 'Finally we killed them all. There was not much jubilation. We just sat and stared at the sand, and most of us thought of those who were gone—those whom I shall remember as always young, smiling and graceful, and I shall try to forget how they looked at the end, beyond all recognition'.[19]

Many other islands and atolls, such as Nauru, Ponape and Jaluit, Mili, Wotje and Maloelap in the Marshalls, were never invaded at all, but simply 'leap-frogged' and neutralized by air strikes from time to time. The loss of such important atolls in the Gilberts and Marshalls, and MacArthur's steady progress in New Guinea, forced the Japanese High Command to abandon the strategy of defending an outer line extending to the Bismarcks, and to set up instead a new, inner defensive line, more than a thousand miles to the west, running from the Marianas, to the Palaus, to western New Guinea. Scores of islands and bases, including Rabaul and Truk, to the east of this line remained in Japanese hands until the very end of the war, but their garrisons, bypassed by the Allied advance and many of them cut off from all assistance except from submarines, were left to wither on the vine, being decimated by starvation, by disease, and by repeated attacks from Fifth Fleet carriers, which used these isolated

Japanese outposts as 'live' practice targets for aircrews new to the Pacific.

In New Guinea, South-west Pacific Command began the new year of 1944 with landings at Saidor on 2 January. A plan for capturing Kavieng in New Ireland was dropped and the invasion of the Admiralty Islands north of New Guinea brought forward when a reconnaissance in force on 29 February, with MacArthur himself present, was turned into a proper invasion. The islands were secured on 24 March. MacArthur then side-stepped the main Japanese 18th Army at Wewak by landing further along the coast at Hollandia and Aitape. For these operations he had the assistance of the Fifth Fleet. Ever more confident of their power to stay at sea within range of Japanese air bases, Task Force 58 steamed south and secured MacArthur's seaward flank in March and April with further strikes at Truk, on the Palau Islands and the western Carolines. Landings at Hollandia were successfully carried out on 22 April, and on the offshore island of Wakde on 17 May. MacArthur's next main target was the large island of Biak. But the landings there, on 27 May, met much stiffer resistance than expected.

Biak was important to Japanese strategy. Its airfields were needed to give land-based air support for the Japanese First Mobile Fleet in Operation A-GO, which was a plan devised by the new C.-in-C. Admiral Soemu Toyoda (Koga had been killed in an air crash in March 1944) to bring the American fleet to decisive action in the area of the western Carolines. A strong naval force under Vice-Admiral Matome Ugaki had begun to assemble at Batjan in the Moluccas to carry out this plan, when, quite suddenly, the whole strategic position for the Japanese was utterly changed by events a thousand miles to the north.

Marines and coastguardmen displaying a Japanese battle flag captured on Eniwetok

On 11 June 1944, 200 Hellcats from TF 58 made a series of fighter
sweeps over the airfields in the Marianas. The next day, two
carrier groups attacked Saipan and Tinian while the third struck
at Guam. On the 13th, seven new battleships under Rear-
Admiral Lee bombarded coastal towns and installations. The
bombardment, though heavy, was none too accurate and was
resumed with much more effect the following day by a team of
older battleships, some of them restored survivors of Pearl
Harbor. The meaning of all this activity became suddenly clear
to the Japanese: the Allies were about to assault the Marianas.

For the Japanese, an attack on the Marianas overrode any
other consideration in the Pacific. Important atolls in the Gilberts
and Marshalls could be lost. Great fortresses like Truk and
Rabaul could, if necessary, be abandoned. But if the Marianas
fell, including Saipan, the naval and adminstrative centre of the
Japanese inner defence ring, then Japan's own defeat would surely
follow.

The decision to attack the Marianas, with a target date of 15
June, was taken by the Joint Chiefs of Staff as late as 12 March.
At that time the main Allied strategic preoccupation was the
imminent invasion of Normandy. But there were still three U.S.
Marine and two U.S. Army divisions in the Pacific, and the
Fifth Fleet was growing stronger every week. The four main
islands, Guam, Saipan, Tinian and Rota (of which the first three
were taken), were centrally placed for further advances west to
the Philippines, north-west to Formosa, or north up the Bonin
and Volcano islands to Japan itself. They would provide advanced
naval bases and airfields for long-range Superfortress bombing
of the Japanese mainland. Last, but not at all least, Guam
belonged to the United States.

The Expeditionary Force had some very familiar names:
Spruance commanded the Fifth Fleet, and Mitscher the fast
carriers. Richmond Kelly Turner, now making his fifth major
amphibious operation, commanded the Joint Expeditionary
Force, with 'Howling Mad' Smith commanding the troops; these
two also commanded the Northern Attack Force, comprising the
2nd and 4th Marine Divisions, mounted in Hawaii and the
American West Coast and intended for Saipan and Tinian. The
Southern Attack Force had 'Close-In' Conolly and Major-
General Roy Geiger U.S.M.C., with the 3rd Marine Division,
mounted in Tulagi and Guadalcanal and aimed at Guam.
Admiral Blandy and General Ralph Smith commanded the
Floating Reserve, comprising the U.S. Army 27th Division.

In time and distance and numbers, the scale of the Marianas
invasion dwarfed anything that had preceded it in the Pacific.
Saipan was more than 3,500 miles from Pearl Harbor, and more
than a thousand even from the nearest advanced base at Eniwetok,
itself only a coral atoll harbour, to which everything for the
assault had to be brought. The distances involved meant that the

121

The flight deck of the U.S. carrier *Enterprise* seen from one of her own aircraft

entire expeditionary force was afloat and on its way at the same time, and the ships concerned were needed for more than three months. But such was the command of sea and air that the Allies had won over such vast areas of the Pacific that the 535 ships for the invasion, carrying or escorting 71,000 troops from Hawaii and another 58,000 from the Solomons, were able to assemble, sail and reach their destinations unharmed. In spite of the vast scale of the operation and the short time allowed, Turner set the date of 15 June, and the 15th it was. The date for Guam was left open, depending upon events.

For an attacker, the Marianas posed all the problems of the coral atolls, and some new ones. Their coasts had the same tidal quirks, coral reefs and shelves. Ashore, the enemy had room for manoeuvre, with mountains and limestone cave complexes ideal for defence. For the first time, the targets were populated by Japanese citizens and people friendly to the Japanese. The Saipan garrison, under Lieutenant-General Yoshitsugu Saito, consisted of 22,000 soldiers of the 43rd Division and 47th Independent Mixed Brigade. Sinkings by American submarines had greatly reduced reinforcements for Saipan but the enemy strength

was still twice that estimated by Allied intelligence. There were also some 7,000 officers and men of the Japanese Navy, under Nagumo—the same Nagumo of Pearl Harbor, but now demoted to a subordinate position. Shore defences, gun emplacements and bunkers were nothing like as strong as they had been for the coral atolls, because until 1944 the Japanese never believed that they would ever have to fortify the Marianas. But the materials were there and, given another three months' construction time, Saipan would have been an even more formidable proposition.

The landings were preceded by most informative photo-reconnaissance flights by specially fitted Navy Liberators flying from Henderson, and by the activities of the new Underwater Demolition Teams. These were expert swimmers, trained to reconnoitre and survey beaches (they actually had black rings, twelve inches apart, painted on their bodies so that they could measure soundings) and later, when covered by naval gunfire, place underwater demolition charges to blast paths through the coral for the landing craft. With such assistance, and with the usual massive air cover and bombardment support, the assault troops were in very good heart, being especially cheered by the news of the D-Day landings in Normandy while they were on their way.

When the sun rose on 15 June the people of Saipan looked out in astonishment at the huge fleet which had materialized offshore overnight. Accompanied by naval guns and ground strafing by cannon-firing Hellcats and rocket-bearing Avengers, some 8,000 Marines were ashore in the first twenty minutes and 20,000 troops were on land by nightfall. That night the Japanese counter-attacked with screaming banzai charges and the assault troops had a sleepless time. But the next morning they were still there. At sea, the Navy hoped that the Japanese fleet would come out.

These hopes were on the point of being realized. In March the Japanese had reorganized their Navy so that virtually 90 per cent of all their seagoing ships except for submarines formed the First Mobile Fleet, under a most able commander, Vice-Admiral Jisaburo Ozawa. On 3 May the C.-in-C. Admiral Soemu Toyoda issued his orders for Operation A-GO, a plan for a 'special force' to lure the American fleet to certain 'designated areas' either off the Palaus or the western Carolines, where it would come within range of the maximum number of Japanese air bases. (There was also the consideration that the Japanese Navy did not have enough fuel to venture much further afield than the 'designated areas'.) The Americans would then be crushed between the 'hammer' of Ozawa's ships and the 'anvil' of land-based air power. As always the Japanese plans were somewhat complicated and relied upon the enemy doing the right thing. But by that stage of the war the Japanese were no longer capable of 'luring' the Allies anywhere, or of imposing any sort of plan upon them. Japan's only hope of success lay in a mistake by Spruance.

In May the First Mobile Fleet assembled at Tawitawi, in the western end of the Sulu Archipelago. There they were well placed for a naval battle in the area chosen by them, and were only 180 miles from the oilfields of Tarakan, whose oil was of such quality that it could be burnt in ships' boilers without intervening refining. But Tawitawi had no airfield on which aircrews could practise and keep their flying edge, and it was an open anchorage where prowling U.S. submarines soon began to pick off targets. At the same time, the Japanese built up their shore-based air power to some 540 aircraft disposed in a great ring from Chichi Jima in the north to New Guinea in the south, with the majority in the south, which would suit the Japanese better, and which they therefore expected would be the most likely place for the Allies to strike.

The same wishful thinking governed their positioning of submarines used, as usual in the Japanese Navy, for scouting rather than direct offence. The Japanese worked out which way the carriers had gone to attack Hollandia, hoped they would do the same again, therefore expected them to, and placed their submarines accordingly in the 'Na' line, running north-east to south-west some 130 miles north of the Admiralty Islands. But intelligence and alert anti-submarine crews soon discovered them and seventeen submarines were sunk, without themselves sinking a single Allied ship or even gaining one useful sighting report.

The most astonishing performance here, and indeed in the whole of the war against Axis submarines, was put up by the destroyer escort U.S.S. *England* (Lieutenant-Commander W. B. Pendleton U.S.N.) who sank six submarines in twelve days in May 1944. Although she was new, with only about ten weeks' experience at sea, *England* was so successful with her ahead-thrown 'Hedgehog' weapons that her task force commander, Commander Hains, eventually held her back to give his other ships a chance. But when their attacks had failed, *England* was called up, moved smoothly in, and nailed the submarine with her Hedgehogs every time. 'Goddammit,' Hains signalled, 'how do you do it?' *England* replied: 'Personnel and equipment worked with the smoothness of well-oiled clockwork. As a result of our efforts, Recording Angel working overtime checking in Nip submariners joining Honourable Ancestors.' From Washington Admiral King, not noted for levity, signalled 'There'll always be an *England* in the United States Navy.'

On 13 June, the day the battlewagons began their pounding of Saipan, Ozawa's First Mobile Fleet sailed from Tawitawi, observed and reported as they went by the U.S. submarine *Redfin*. Rear-Admiral Ugaki, who had taken a force including the two monster battleships *Yamato* and *Musashi* south to assist the hard-pressed army in Biak, was recalled and sailed from Batjan the same day. Receiving *Redfin's* report, Spruance calculated that it would be the 17th before the enemy could be in position, so he

allowed Rear-Admiral 'Jocko' Clark to race 650 miles north-westwards with two carrier groups to destroy aircraft at Chichi Jima and Iwo Jima on 15 and 16 June. These aircraft would otherwise have been staged through to reinforce Guam and Saipan.

Ozawa's ships were sighted and reported emerging from the San Bernardino Strait by the U.S. submarine *Flying Fish* at 6.35 p.m. on the 15th, and an hour later *Seahorse* sighted Ugaki's battleships steaming northwards, about 200 miles east-south-east of the Surigao Strait. So Spruance knew that two enemy forces were heading towards him; but, incredibly, these submarine sightings were the last enemy reports he was to get for a very long time, although a third submarine, *Cavalla*, reported oilers and destroyers early on the 17th.

Ugaki's ships met the First Mobile Fleet at 4 p.m. on the 16th, about 300 miles east of the Philippines. In battle order, Ozawa had his ships in three groups. A van force under Vice-Admiral Takeo Kurita, had three light carriers, *Chitose*, *Chiyoda* and *Zuiho*, with eighty-eight aircraft under Rear-Admiral Sueo Obayashi, escorted by the battleships *Yamato*, *Musashi*, *Haruna* and *Kongo*, four heavy cruisers, and destroyers. This force was some 100 miles ahead of the main fleet, which was in two groups: 'A' Group, under Ozawa himself, with his flag in the new carrier *Taiho*, and *Shokaku* and *Zuikaku*, carrying 207 aircraft, escorted by cruisers and destroyers; and 'B' Group, under Rear-Admiral Takaji Joshima, with the carriers *Junyo* and *Hiyo* and the light carrier *Ryuho*, with 135 aircraft, escorted by the battleship *Nagato*, one cruiser, and destroyers. It was hoped that Kurita's van would act as 'bait' and draw the enemy on to the main fleet. If that happened, it would be a climactic moment in the Pacific War, as Ozawa well knew. He made the signal Admiral Togo had made to his fleet before Tsushima nearly forty years earlier: 'The fate of the Empire rests on this one battle. Every man is expected to do his utmost.'

Between Ozawa and Saipan lay Spruance's Task Force 58, a vast armada thirty-five miles by twenty-five, covering an area of 700 square miles of sea, with fifteen carriers, 965 aircraft, seven battleships, twenty-one cruisers and sixty-nine destroyers. The carrier groups were: TG 58.1 (Clark): *Hornet* and *Yorktown*, with the light carriers *Belleau Wood* and *Bataan*; TG 58.2 (Rear-Admiral Montgomery): *Bunker Hill* and *Wasp*, with light carriers *Monterey* and *Cabot*; TG 58.3 (Rear-Admiral Reeves): *Enterprise* and *Lexington*, with *Princeton* and *San Jacinto*; and TG 58.4 (Rear-Admiral Harrill): *Essex*, with *Langley* and *Cowpens*. Mitscher flew his flag in *Lexington*, Spruance in the heavy cruiser *Indianapolis*. Even at this stage of the war, even such a brilliant employer of air power as Spruance evidently had a vestigial, almost atavastic, belief in the battleship as the ultimate arbiter of naval battles; a special battle group, TG 58.7, was formed under Lee, with

Washington, North Carolina, Iowa, New Jersey, South Dakota, Alabama and *Indiana*. No battleship came within 300 miles of an enemy at any time during the battle and Harrill's carrier group had to stand by to cover them.

Ozawa had carefully planned his approach so as to elude air search but, in any case, although Spruance's fleet was so superior to the Japanese in almost every way, it was markedly inferior in air search. TF 58's searches and those of land-based aircraft were in general too few, too short and mostly wrongly aimed. But *Cavalla*'s report on the 17th showed that the Japanese were still standing on, and Mitscher suggested a night battleship action, with a possible air strike at first light on the 18th. Lee refused, probably sharing Spruance's view that their greatest danger was an outflanking 'end run' by Ozawa.

Much better served by air reconnaissance, Ozawa received two really good sighting reports on the afternoon of the 18th, one pilot having seen the northern end of TF 58 and the other the southern. Ozawa's plan had always been to make use of his aircraft's greater striking range by keeping a minimum of 300 miles from his enemy. Now, he made the important decision to steer away and attack the next morning, having his van at 300 and his main body at 400 miles range from Spruance. Obayashi in the van force began to launch a strike of sixty-seven aircraft on his own initiative, but on receiving Ozawa's signal of his intention to attack in the morning he cancelled his strike and recalled the aircraft that had taken off. This was a chance lost. A strike then, arriving at dusk, might well have caught TF 58 off guard and done some damage.

Meanwhile, Spruance had received an intelligence report from Pearl Harbor, based on direction-finding bearings, which put the Japanese fleet some 350 miles west-south-west of him. Spruance might have turned back. Mitscher thought he should have turned back. Mitscher, whose only responsibility was for his carriers and whose only thought was to ward off any danger to them, suggested TF 58 steam west so as to be ready to strike early on the 19th. Spruance thought about it for over an hour and then rejected the suggestion. Spruance had responsibility for the whole operation. His instructions were to capture, occupy and defend Saipan and he allowed nothing, neither the prospect of defeating the Japanese fleet, nor the fear of being 'shuttle-bombed' by Japanese carrier aircraft which attacked and then landed ashore to rearm and refuel, to deflect him from his main purpose. Spruance had always in mind the fear of Ozawa's 'end run'. Ironically, a search aircraft obtained a radar contact early the next morning which confirmed the direction-finder's estimate of the Japanese fleet's position. But the report was not received for some eight hours. Even had Spruance received it earlier, he probably would have acted no differently. As it happened, he had TF 58 perfectly positioned to take the Japanese onslaught

which sporadic air activity on the night of 18/19 June showed
could not be far off.

For one reason or another, all the U.S. air searches had failed
to find the Japanese fleet and when 19 June dawned Spruance
still had only the stale submarine and intelligence reports of
where his enemy lay. The day's action began with fighter sweeps
over Guam, Rota, Tinian and Saipan, in which Japanese aircraft
on the ground were shot up and aircraft in the air were shot
down, including some reinforcements from Truk. With the losses
they had already suffered, the Japanese anvil, on which they had
placed such hopes, was shattered before the main battle had
opened. (Jocko Clark's strikes, and the Japanese belief that
Mitscher would attack Yap or the Paluas, had in any case caused
the Japanese to bring fewer aircraft to the Marianas.)

Ozawa began flying off searches at 4.45 a.m., well before dawn.
Some were shot down, but Ozawa soon had reports of part of
TF 58's great array of ships. By 8.30 Obayashi was flying off the
first Japanese strike of the day: forty-five Zekes with bombs,
eight Jills with torpedoes, escorted by sixteen Zekes. They were
detected by radar at about 150 miles range. The fighter direction
officers of TF 58 had time and scope to deploy the Hellcats, who
had space and height enough to intercept. The Hellcat pilots
were experienced men, who had been flying for two years and
had more than 300 hours. According to them, their opponents
were mostly greenhorns, with a few old hands as stiffening. These
were not the hardened veterans of Nagumo's day. These raw
crews broke their formations prematurely, sacrificing precious
collective security, made elementary errors in formation flying,
fell for the simplest attacking ruses, and, worst of all, failed to
press home or co-ordinate their attacks properly. It was not a
contest but a massacre. Only twenty-four of that raid survived,
having scored one bomb hit on *South Dakota* (as it turned out, the
only TF 58 ship hit that day).

Ozawa's second raid was a big one, of fifty-three Judy bombers,
twenty-seven Jill torpedo-bombers and forty-eight Zeke fighters,
launched from Ozawa's own division of large carriers at 9 a.m.
As the flagship *Taiho* was steaming up into the wind to launch
aircraft, she was hit by one of a salvo of six torpedoes from the
U.S. submarine *Albacore*; she might have been hit again but for an
extraordinary act of self-sacrifice by Warrant Officer Sakio
Komatsu, who had just taken off when he saw the torpedo's track
and crashed his Zeke on top of it. No serious damage appeared
to have been done to *Taiho*, and her speed was only reduced by
one knot.

Eight of the strike returned prematurely, and two were shot
down by 'friendly' fire as they flew over Kurita's force. The
remainder had an even hotter reception over TF 58. Although
one or two of the carriers were near-missed and a torpedo-
bomber crashed into *Indiana*, fortunately without exploding its

torpedo, ninety-seven of the aircraft in this raid never returned to their carriers. As *Shokaku* was landing on the pitifully few survivors of her air group, she herself was hit by three torpedoes from the U.S. submarine *Cavalla*. *Shokaku* fell out of line and began to lose power. Explosions started fires which, as in her predecessors at Midway, were spread by petrol. Just after 3 p.m. a bomb magazine detonated, tearing *Shokaku* apart. In *Cavalla*, the crew heard the explosions, and the prolonged ominous rumblings of the ship breaking up.

Shokaku was quickly followed by *Taiho*. That single torpedo had damaged her petrol tanks, and the vapour was spread through the ship through an inexperienced damage control officer opening up ship's ventilation. Fumes from the crude Tarakan fuel were added to the petrol. *Taiho* soon became a giant petrol bomb awaiting a spark. It came just after 3.30 with an explosion which lifted the armoured flight deck and blew out the hangar sides and the very hull-plates in the bottom of the ship. Ozawa and the Emperor's portrait were transferred to a destroyer and then to the cruiser *Haguro*. Only about 500 of *Taiho's* crew of 2,150 were saved.

The third raid of twenty-five Zekes with bombs, seven Jills and fifteen escort Zekes was flown off from *Junyo* and *Hiyo* at 10 a.m. They were directed to a false sighting position and, fortunately for them, missed TF 58. Only about a dozen of them were engaged and seven shot down.

The fourth and last strike, another big one of thirty Zekes, nine Judys, twenty-seven Vals, six Jills and ten Zeke fighter-bombers, began taking off from *Junyo*, *Hiyo*, *Ryuho* and *Zuikaku* at 11 a.m. After first flying to a phantom contact south-west of Guam, they turned north. Once again, the interpretative skills of TF 58's fighter direction teams matched the aggressive flying of the Hellcat pilots. Six Judys who attacked one carrier group did no damage and were all shot down except one. Eighteen more aircraft were intercepted by Hellcats and only half survived. Forty-nine remnants, trying to land on Guam, were caught by twenty-seven Hellcats from *Cowpens*, *Essex* and *Hornet* and thirty of them were shot down. Another nineteen were lost operationally and in deck-landing crashes. So only nine of the eighty-two on that strike ever returned, and none of them had done any damage to TF 58.

Throughout the day a fighter sweep from *Yorktown* patrolled Guam, and TF 58's bombers, which had flown off to keep clear, raided airfields on all the islands, bombing cripples and generally keeping the enemy quiescent. In the eight and a half hours' hectic flying of what the U.S. bluejackets later came to call 'the Great Marianas Turkey Shoot', Ozawa lost two carriers and 346 aircraft. TF 58 had lost thirty aircraft, and had suffered one hit on *Indiana*. If the Coral Sea had been a battle in which no ship sighted an enemy ship, then the 'Turkey Shoot' was the day the

U.S. Navy scored a great victory without one ship or aircraft ever sighting an enemy.

The victory might have been greater, for at this point an opportunity was lost. Incredibly, TF 58 flew no searches that night of the 19th/20th. Possibly Mitscher thought his aircrews had done enough for one day, or conceivably there was some lingering 'mental block' in the carrier groups about night-flying. As it was, the first search flight next morning at 5.30 was some seventy-five miles short of Ozawa's ships, milling about and preparing to refuel for another day's operations.

For Ozawa had by no means given up. Huddled with his staff in a cramped cabin under *Haguro's* bridge, and with only her limited communications systems at his disposal, he still had no clear idea of what had happened. He knew he had lost two carriers and many of the aircraft had not returned, but they had probably landed on Guam for the night. Vice-Admiral Kakuta,

U.S. Marines hugging the beach while land mines explode nearby on Guam

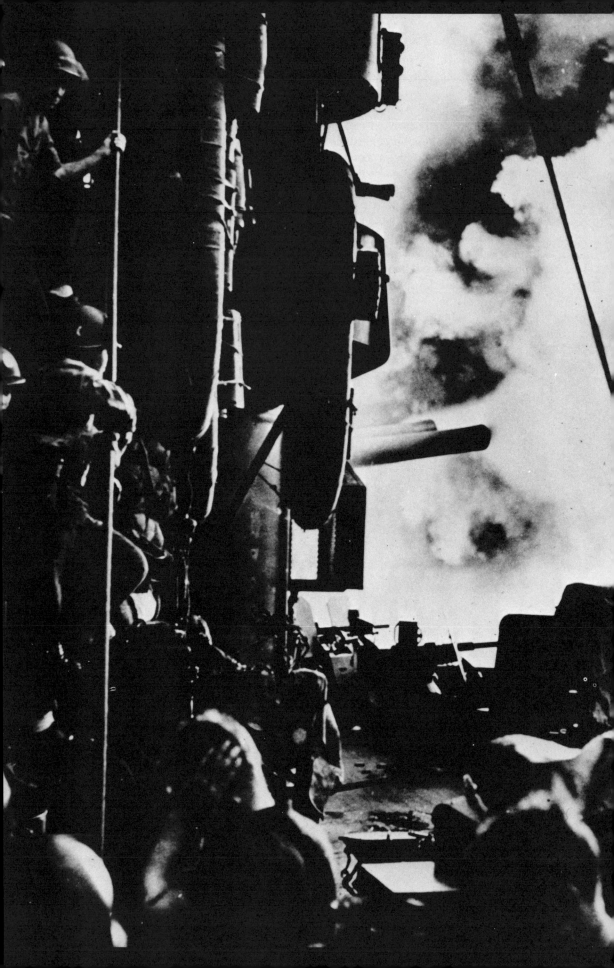

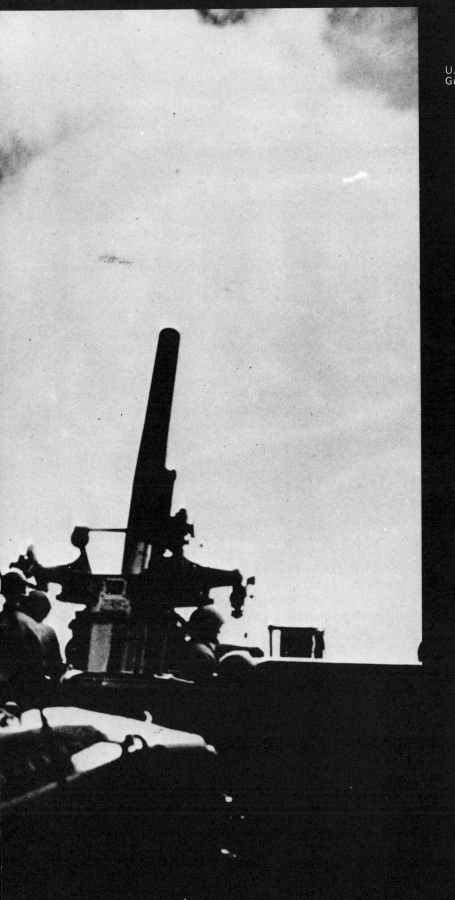

U.S. naval bombardment of
Guam, July 1944

133

commanding the base air force in the Marianas from Tinian, consistently under-reported his losses. Even when he shifted his flag to *Zuikaku* Ozawa was still unaware, as Yamamoto had been at Midway, of the catastrophe that had befallen the Japanese Navy.

There was more to come. Ozawa's ships were sighted at last at 4 p.m. on the 20th. This was the first sighting of the enemy by a TF 58 aircraft in the whole battle. The range was 275 miles. Dusk was at 7 p.m. It was very late, but not too late. Mitscher decided on an all-out strike. A full deckload—eighty-five Hellcats, seventy-seven Helldivers, and fifty-four torpedo-Avengers from *Hornet*, *Yorktown*, *Bunker Hill*, *Wasp*, *Enterprise*, *Belleau Wood*, *Bataan*, *Monterey*, *Cabot* and *San Jacinto*—was launched in the astonishing time of ten minutes.

There was no time for the niceties of co-ordinating attacks. The strike had to get in and out before darkness fell. In such hurried circumstances they did very well, sinking the light carrier *Hiyo*, damaging *Chiyoda* with one bomb hit and sinking two tankers. The resistance put up by Ozawa's combat air patrol (C.A.P.) confirmed the Hellcat pilots' suspicions that only the greenhorns had been chopped down over TF 58 and the veterans had survived. But, with further losses, Ozawa had only thirty operational aircraft left at the end of the day, out of the 450 with which he had begun the battle. After ordering Kurita to carry out a surface engagement, and then cancelling it, Ozawa recognized defeat and, like Yamamoto, turned for home. On the way he he signalled his resignation to Japan.

Complete darkness had fallen before TF 58's strike returned to their carriers. Every carrier and every ship in the screen turned on masthead lights, deck lighting and red and green navigation lights and flashed signalling lights until, as one pilot said, the fleet looked like 'a Mardi Gras setting fantastically out of place here, midway between the Marianas and the Philippines'. Recovery took two hours. Aircraft ran out of fuel yards away from their carriers and landed in the sea. Others landed on where they could, on the wrong carriers or even on carriers which tried desperately to wave them off because their deck was cluttered. Many of the ditched aircrews were picked up next day and on subsequent days. TF 58 lost a total of 130 aircraft on 19 and 20 June and 76 aircrew, compared with the Japanese losses of 476 aircraft and about 445 aircrew.

Spruance began a stern chase that evening but it was quickly obvious that the enemy was outdistancing him and he called off the chase at 7.20 p.m. on 21 June. The invasion of Saipan could now go on without interruption and the island was secured on 9 July after a bitter campaign. General Saito committed suicide as did Admiral Nagumo. The victor of Pearl Harbor, and the man who had taken Japanese arms across the world from Hawaii to the shores of India, shot himself in a cave and was buried in an unmarked grave. Nor did the Japanese civilian population surrender. In a horrifying conclusion to the campaign, hundreds of men, women and children committed suicide by throwing themselves off the cliffs of Marpi Point, the north end of the island. Parents dashed out their babies' brains before jumping. Brothers tossed hand grenades to their little sisters. Fathers slit mothers' throats. Even those who wanted to live were threatened by surviving Japanese soldiers and jumped with the rest.

Tinian was invaded, after days of heavy bombardment, on 24 July and secured by 2 August, although mopping up of small parties went on for months. The date for the Guam invasion had been postponed when Spruance heard of the approach of the Japanese fleet on 16 June. It finally took place, after thirteen days' bombardment, on 21 July and the island was recovered by 12 August.

The successes of *Cavalla* and *Albacore* were not known for some time and there was some disappointment at Pearl Harbor over the outcome of the battle in the Philippine Sea. Spruance was criticized for not taking the offensive on 18 June or chasing more vigorously on the 20th. Eventually even Spruance himself seems to have been persuaded that somehow the battle had not been conclusive. In fact, by staying on the defensive on the 19th and letting the enemy come to him, Spruance had won a smashing victory. In Spruance's hand, the Hellcat fighter had been a trump-card. Some Japanese carriers had escaped but they were neutered animals without their air groups. The Japanese carriers were never a force again and the next time they were used in battle it was only as almost impotent bait.

U.S. infantrymen wading ashore from L.S.T.s at Saipan

9 THE BATTLE OF LEYTE GULF

Prelude to Leyte—heavy columns of smoke from naval gun bombardment and carrier aircraft strikes, 20 October 1944

Events in the Pacific now hurried towards the largest battle in naval history, the second of that year in the Philippine Sea, known as the Battle of Leyte Gulf, although it was in fact four separate major engagements. This was the *coup de grâce* for the Imperial Japanese Navy. They were never again a navy, in any strategic sense of the word. But although nothing could have won the war for Japan at that stage, a Japanese decoy plan for once worked perfectly and, with a little more luck and a little more resolution, it might have delayed the Allied invasion of the Philippines for many months.

The Joint Chiefs of Staff's directive of 12 March 1944 had ordered Nimitz to take the Marianas, and then to occupy the Palau Islands. MacArthur meanwhile was to have the support of the Pacific Fleet for landings at Mindanao preparatory to a further advance to Formosa, either direct or by way of Luzon. MacArthur naturally insisted that the Allies were honour-bound to liberate the Philippines, and the differences between the 'Army' and the 'Navy' strategies reached their bitterest point. But despite personal arbitration by Roosevelt at Honolulu in July 1944, in which he showed himself in sympathy with Mac-Arthur's case, the final shape of the Allied assault on Japan was still unsettled by the time of the Octagon Conference at Quebec in September 1944.

With MacArthur's forces already at Sansapor, on the western tip of New Guinea, and Nimitz in the Marianas, the two arms of the Allied offensive in the Pacific were only a thousand miles apart, poised to strike at Luzon or at Formosa. Before the Mindanao landing on 15 November, MacArthur planned to invade Morotai on 15 September and the Talaud Islands a month later, building airfields on both so that he could advance always under cover of land-based fighters. Nimitz decided to assault the Palaus, also on 15 September, and go on to take Yap, as an additional airfield against Truk, and Ulithi, for development as an advanced fleet base. These programmes were presented to the Combined Chiefs of Staff's Committee at Quebec.

Meanwhile, the Fast Carrier Task Force was at sea, carrying out softening-up strikes on Yap, the Palaus, Mindanao and the central Philippine Islands. The fleet commander was now Halsey. On 15 June 1944 the Pacific Fleet command had been reorganized to match the accelerating tempo of the war. Halsey had been relieved as C.-in-C. South Pacific and appointed to command the Pacific Fleet, alternating with Spruance. While one admiral and his staff were embarked, the others were ashore planning the next operation. Thus Spruance commanded in the Gilberts, Marshalls, Marianas, Iwo and the Ryukyus; Halsey, in the western Carolines, the Philippines and in the final strikes against the Japanese mainland. The ships remained the same, only the nomenclature was changed: the fleet was the Fifth under Spruance, the Third under Halsey, the Fast Carrier Task Force

137

TF 58 under Spruance, TF 38 under Halsey. As Nimitz said, 'the team remains about the same, but the drivers change.'

Halsey's September strikes met startlingly little opposition, because the Japanese were husbanding their resources until they saw the Allies plainly committed to a major offensive in the Philippines. Some two hundred Japanese aircraft were destroyed, and several ships, for the loss of eight aircraft from TF 38. Excited, and convinced that the central Philippines were just 'a hollow shell with weak defenses and skimpy facilities', Halsey urgently suggested to Nimitz that the planned assaults on Yap and the Palaus be cancelled and everything concentrated upon an early invasion of Leyte.

Nimitz agreed to bypass Yap but demurred about missing the Palaus. So, after the familiar and well-drilled overtures of air strike and bombardment by TF 38, the 1st U.S. Marine Division went ashore on Peleliu, 470 miles east of Mindanao, on 15 September. The Japanese garrison of 10,000 troops, including the 14th Division, were as strongly esconced in natural caves and interlocking fortifications as anywhere in the Pacific and the battle was fully as bitter as anything that had gone before. Organized Japanese resistance did not end until early in 1945.

Peleliu was probably an unnecessary acquisition, and the assault was one of Nimitz's rare errors. But the neighbouring atoll of Ulithi had been abandoned by the Japanese and was taken without opposition on 23 September. Although somewhat vulnerable to typhoons, Ulithi had a superb natural harbour and quickly became the Third Fleet's main advanced base.

MacArthur's forces had meanwhile bypassed a strong Japanese garrison at Halmahera in the Moluccas, and landed virtually unopposed on the more northerly island of Morotai. By the beginning of October 1944, the Allies held an inner ring of islands running south from the Marianas to the Moluccas and were in position to assault the Philippines. At Quebec the Joint Chiefs of Staff considered the implications of Halsey's news. The landings at Yap, the Talauds and Mindanao were cancelled. Nimitz and MacArthur were ordered to join forces for a landing at Leyte on 20 October, two months before the date originally set for an invasion of the Philippines. Such was the flexibility of the Allies' planning, and so wide the options open to them, that the 24th Army Corps, then actually embarked for the Yap assault, was diverted to Manus in the Admiralty Islands to join MacArthur's force for Leyte. After Leyte an invasion of Luzon was inevitable, and indeed the Chiefs of Staff ordered MacArthur, in a directive of 3 October, to invade Luzon on a target date of 20 December 1944, and then to support Nimitz's subsequent invasion of the Ryukyus. Nimitz, similarly, was ordered to support MacArthur's operations in Luzon, occupy an island in the Bonins, with a target date of 20 January 1945, and an island in the Ryukyus, with a target date of 1 March 1945. Thus the long argument between the 'Army' and 'Navy' plans was finally resolved by the pace and pressure of events. But, even now, Roosevelt neglected to appoint one man, either MacArthur or Nimitz, as supreme commander in the Pacific. This divided command was to have nearly fatal results off Leyte.

On 10 October TF 38's fifteen carriers began preliminary strikes in support of the Leyte landings. The attacks were so widespread, from the Ryukyus down to the northern Philippines, and so heavy, with up to a thousand aircraft taking part, that the Japanese were convinced that the main assault was underway. This belief was strengthened on Friday 13 October, south of Formosa, when Japanese aircraft penetrated TF 38's screen and hit the heavy cruiser U.S.S. *Canberra* with one torpedo. The next day they scored another hit, on the light cruiser *Houston*. Returning Japanese airmen vastly overestimated their successes, claiming to have sunk two battleships and eleven carriers and damaged many other ships. Radio Tokyo made the most of this news and the Japanese Navy appeared to believe their own propaganda, for Vice-Admiral Shima, with the heavy cruisers *Nachi* and *Ashigara*, and destroyer escort, were sent out to mop up the 'cripples'. In fact, Halsey was using the two damaged cruisers as 'bait', but Shima realized this and withdrew in time. By notable seamanship and damage control, the two badly damaged ships were towed clear, and on the 19th Nimitz was able to counter Japanese propaganda with the joyful message that 'Admiral Halsey is now retiring towards the enemy following the salvage of all the Third Fleet ships recently reported sunk by Radio Tokyo.'

The loss of the Philippines would effectively cut off Japan from the resources of the Dutch East Indies and Malaya. The Japanese had a plan—codenamed SHO 1—for the defence of the Philippines, which Admiral Toyoda, in Tokyo, prematurely activated. He committed hundreds of land-based and naval aircraft to the Philippines, where they were severely mauled by TF 38's aircraft. The Japanese lost some 500 aircraft in trying to stop an invasion which had not yet begun.

However, that invasion was imminent. In the early hours of 20 October, after a two-day bombardment, the first assault troops went ashore on Leyte beaches, meeting very slight opposition. The Japanese Navy first heard of the invasion force on the 17th, and put into operation their own part of SHO 1, which as usual had a complicated command structure involving several detached forces and a decoy.

At that time, the surviving heavy ships of the Japanese Navy were mostly based at Singapore, because it was nearer their fuel supplies and because Truk was now impossible as a base. The surviving carriers meanwhile were based in Japan, attempting to train up fresh air groups to replace those massacred in the Philippine Sea in June. On 18 October Vice-Admiral Takeo Kurita sailed from Lingga Roads, off Singapore, with the First Striking Force, calling at Brunei on the 22nd to refuel. After leaving Brunei, this force split into two. Kurita's Force 'A' (known to the Allies as Centre Force) was itself in two sections; the first, under Kurita himself, with the battleships *Yamato*, *Musashi* and *Nagato*, six heavy cruisers with Kurita flying his flag in *Atago*, the light cruiser *Noshiro* and nine destroyers; the second, under Vice-Admiral Yoshio Suzuki, with the battleships *Kongo* and *Haruna*, four heavy cruisers, the light cruiser *Yahagi* and six destroyers. Both these sections headed for the Sibuyan Sea and, ultimately, the San Bernardino Strait. Force 'C' (Southern Force), under Vice-Admiral Shoji Nishimura, with battleships *Yamashiro* and *Fuso*, the heavy cruiser *Mogami* and three destroyers, headed for the Surigao Strait. Nishimura was to be reinforced by Shima's two heavy cruisers, but Shima was to act independently, and the two forces in fact never met.

At the same time, Ozawa's main body (Northern Force) sailed from Japan with four carriers, *Zuikaku*, *Zuiho*, *Chitose* and *Chiyoda*, the two hybrid battleship-carriers *Ise* and *Hyuga*, the light cruisers *Isuku*, *Oyodo* and *Tama*, nine destroyers, some escort vessels and oilers. Ozawa's was really only a shadow force. The four carriers had only 116 aircraft between them, half their normal strength, and the two hybrids had none at all. Ozawa was sailing on a voyage of self-sacrifice, offering his ships as live bait, in the hope of drawing Halsey's carriers away from Leyte Gulf whilst the Japanese capital ships penetrated the Philippine archipelago, Kurita through the San Bernardino, Nishimura and Shima through the Surigao, to emerge upon the eastern side and fall upon the Leyte troop anchorages. This time, the bait was taken—hook, line and sinker.

Early on 23 October, when Kurita's ships were passing through the Palawan Passage, they were sighted and attacked by U.S. submarines *Darter* and *Dace*, who sank *Atago* and *Maya* and damaged another heavy cruiser *Takao* so badly that she had to return to Singapore, where she took no further part in the war (in July 1945 she was attacked where she lay by a British midget submarine). Kurita transferred his flag to *Yamato* and continued eastward. *Darter* later ran aground and became a total loss, her ship's company being taken off in *Dace*.

Early on 24 October land-based Japanese aircraft launched a determined attack on Rear-Admiral Sherman's Task Group 38.3 during which *Princeton* was hit. When the cruiser *Birmingham* went alongside her to render assistance the torpedo stowage in *Princeton*

The U.S. carrier *Princeton* burning after Japanese dive-bomb attack, 24 October 1944

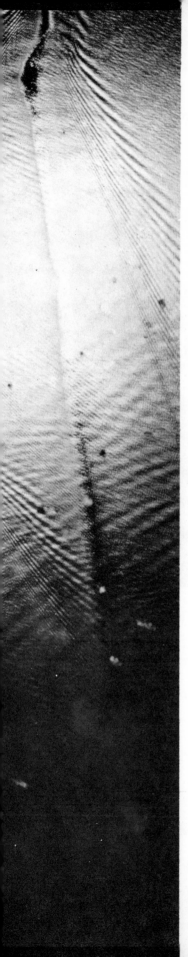

exploded, sweeping *Birmingham's* crowded upper decks with a hail of steel splinters and causing terrible casualties. *Princeton* was abandoned and sunk by torpedoes from the cruiser *Reno*.

Kurita's force was sighted that morning at 8.10 in the Sibuyan Sea and the first of many heavy attacks, launched from Rear-Admiral Bogan's Task Group 38.2 (*Intrepid, Hancock, Bunker Hill, Cabot* and *Independence*), reached it at about 10.30, scoring hits on *Musashi*. She continued to be the main target and, dropping out of line, was soon twenty miles behind Kurita's other ships. Kurita had only a handful of aircraft as cover; these were soon brushed aside, and although all his ships were heavily armed for anti-aircraft fire (the battleships even used their main armament against aircraft at ranges of ten miles) only eighteen U.S. aircraft were shot down out of the hundreds which attacked. Some 259 sorties were flown against Kurita's force that day, with Rear-Admiral Ralph Davison's Task Group 38.4 (*Franklin, Enterprise, San Jacinto* and *Belleau Wood*) also joining in. *Musashi* suffered a total of nineteen torpedo and seventeen assorted bomb hits between 10.30 and 3.20 p.m. but she took a long time to die. She eventually rolled over and sank at 7.35, taking with her 1,023 of her company of 2,287 men. *Miyoko* had damage to two shafts and had to retire, but Kurita's three remaining battleships and his heavy cruisers, though some had been hit, still had their fighting capacity intact.

The American pilots were just as liable to overestimate their successes as the Japanese, and when at 3 p.m. Kurita reversed course to the west, it seemed that his Centre Force had been so badly knocked about that it was limping away from the battle. In fact, Kurita had retired to avoid further air attack and to give land-based aircraft a chance to counter-attack. But Vice-Admiral Fukudome's land-based squadrons had shot their bolt and in any case had concentrated upon attacking the American carrier groups at sea rather than providing badly needed CAPs over Kurita. Realising that the SHO plan was now behind schedule, Kurita turned back to the east again at 5.14 p.m. at 25 knots and an hour later had a signal from Toyoda: 'All forces will attack, trusting in divine guidance.' At 8.20 p.m. Kurita heard from Nishimura that he expected to pass through the Surigao Strait at 4 a.m. the next day, the 25th. He arranged a rendezvous with him ten miles north-east of Suluan at 9 a.m.

Nishimura never kept that rendezvous. His force, and Shima's, had both been sighted by carrier aircraft by noon that day, and a reception had been prepared. Nishimura had no air support or cover whatsoever and clearly would prefer to enter the Surigao Strait after dark and, if brought to action, fight by night. Vice-Admiral Kinkaid, the Seventh Fleet commander, rightly guessed this, and that afternoon of the 24th ordered Rear-Admiral Jesse B. Oldendorf, commanding the Seventh Fleet fire support and bombardment ships, to prepare to meet the enemy. Olden-

Japanese ships evading air attack, Leyte Gulf

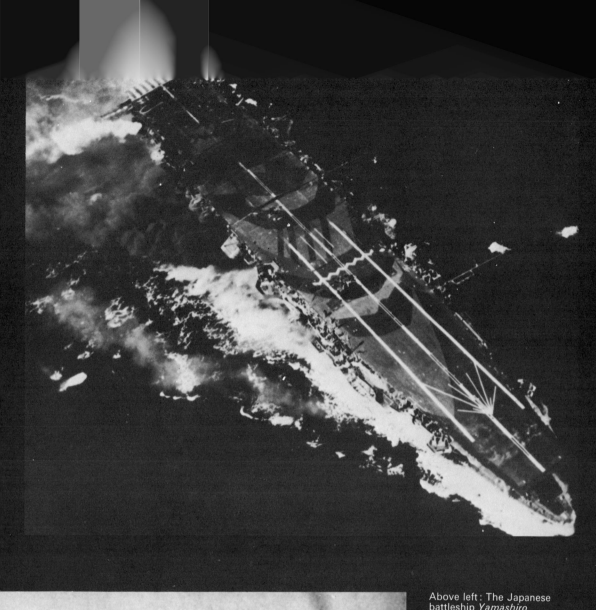

Above left: The Japanese battleship *Yamashiro* (foreground) with the cruiser *Mogami* under air attack by U.S. aircraft in the Sulu Sea, 24 October 1944

Above: The Japanese aircraft carrier *Zuiho* during the battle of Cape Engano. *Zuiho* was sunk shortly after this photograph was taken

Left: Helldivers from the U.S. carrier *Hancock* attacking a *Mogami*-class cruiser, 26 October 1944

'They were expendable'—U.S. Navy P.T. boats at speed

dorf, on the principle of 'never giving a sucker an even break', disposed an overwhelming weight of naval firepower across the fifteen-mile entrance of the straits: six battleships (five of them Pearl Harbor survivors with scores to settle), four heavy cruisers including the Australian H.M.A.S. *Shropshire*, and four light cruisers. He also had at his disposal several divisions of destroyers, and some forty PT boats.

It was the PT boats who first detected Nishimura's ships, shortly after 10 p.m. They were driven off, but others took their place. For fifty miles the PT boats snapped at the battleships' heels, running in at high speed though brightly illuminated by Japanese starshells and searchlights, firing torpedoes and breaking off under gunfire to retire behind their own smokescreens. The PT boats scored no hits but their enemy sighting and action reports by radio gave the waiting Oldendorf what amounted to a running commentary on the enemy's progress towards him.

The last PT boats were chased away at about 2 a.m. on the 25th and for about three-quarters of an hour Nishimura's ships steamed quietly onwards. But at 3 a.m. the destroyer divisions, for once in the war being used in their classical role in a night attack against larger units, began their torpedo runs from port and starboard. Five destroyers of Captain Jesse Coward's Squadron (Desron 54) hit *Fuso* with one torpedo, so that she sheered out of line, burning and exploding; sank the destroyer *Yamagumo*; disabled the destroyer *Michishio*; knocked the bow off another destroyer, *Asagumo*; and finally put one torpedo into *Yamashiro*, in what Oldendorf called a 'brilliantly conceived and well

146

executed attack'. Captain McManes's Desron 24 followed and sank *Michishio*, also hitting *Yamashiro* again but without slowing her down. Nishimura still pressed on, disregarding losses and distractions, apparently determined to reach Leyte Gulf and join Kurita, come what may. He now had only *Yamashiro*, the heavy cruiser *Mogami* and one destroyer, *Shigure*, left.

Nishimura's three remaining ships formed the short stubby pillar of a T, of which Oldendorf's battle line was the enormous, top-heavy cross-bar. No admiral in naval history ever had his T crossed more thoroughly or devastatingly than Nishimura that night in the Surigao Strait. Oldendorf's battlewagons opened fire by radar at 3.50 a.m., range 22,800 yards, closing. Nishimura still came on, into an incredible barrage of tracer and armour-piercing shell of all calibres from the battleships' 16- and 14-inch down to the light cruisers' 6-inch. *Shigure* soon retired, followed by *Mogami*, who was hit several times, fired a salvo of torpedoes, came to a dead stop, got under way again and escaped. *Yamashiro* was soon on fire from end to end, the fires burning so brightly that they silhouetted the great pagoda structure of her upper-works, but she answered fire for some time, scoring hits on one destroyer. *Yamashiro* survived until shortly after 4 a.m., when the destroyer *Newcomb* hit her with two torpedoes. She sank at about 4.20, taking with her Nishimura and all but a tiny handful of her crew.

Shima, following behind Nishimura's ships but not in contact with them, took no part in the action. He sighted the two burning and sinking halves of *Fuso*, but thought he was still approaching Nishimura's van force. He was given no help by *Shigure*, returning from the battle; in an amazing example of Japanese navy protocol, her captain volunteered no information about the battle, explaining after the war that he 'was under Nishimura, not Shima'. After *Nachi* and *Ashigara* had both fired a salvo of torpedoes and *Nachi* had collided with *Mogami*, Shima retired, showing unusual prudence and discretion for a Japanese admiral, until the situation became clearer. Actually, he never returned.

Somewhat belatedly, Oldendorf's cruisers set off in pursuit after 4 a.m., caught up with the seemingly indestructible *Mogami* and finally dispatched her. Aircraft from Sprague's escort carriers off Samar and Army bombers joined in the 'mopping up phase' in which the light cruiser *Abukuma* was sunk. Of all Nishimura's ships, only *Shigure* returned safely to Brunei.

At 35 minutes after midnight on 25 October, Kurita's ships emerged on the eastern side of the San Bernardino Strait. There was no opposition. Sea and sky were clear. No aircraft or radar set or coast-watcher gave the alarm. Marvellously, miraculously, Ozawa's great ruse had worked. Though Kurita did not know it, there was now nothing between him and the Leyte troop anchorages except a few of Vice-Admiral Sprague's small escort carriers.

Admiral Halsey, flying his flag in the battleship *New Jersey*, had spent most of the 24th wondering where Ozawa's carriers were. He was sure they were at sea. It was believed that it was Ozawa's aircraft that had attacked *Princeton* that morning. Honour, past frustration, his reputation as 'scourge of the Japs', his criticisms of what he called Spruance's failure to get the Jap carriers in the Philippine Sea, all made Halsey give the Japanese carriers priority as targets. To a certain extent he was obsessed by them, so that their destruction blotted out all other considerations from his mind.

Ozawa's aircraft had indeed taken part in the morning strike on Sherman's group. A few had been shot down, but most had landed on airfields on Luzon. Ozawa, though he only had thirty serviceable aircraft left with him, was just as anxious to be detected. At 2.30 p.m. he sent Rear-Admiral Matsuda southwards with the two 'hybrids' *Ise* and *Hyuga*, publicly instructing them to engage targets offered to them but privately hoping they would be sighted, as indeed they finally were at 3.40. Ozawa's Main Body was also sighted, about an hour later.

Now, at last, Halsey had the information he wanted. He was no man to sit idly by, watching what he called the 'rathole' of the San Bernardino, hoping his enemy would come out, when his main opponent had been sighted to the north. He was warned that Kurita was once more steering eastwards, but he ignored the warning, sure that Kurita could no longer be a danger after the hammering he had received. At 8.20 p.m. Halsey ordered Bogan's TG 38.2 and Davison's TG 38.4 to steam north, join Sherman's TG 38.3 and attack Ozawa. McCain's TG 38.1, then returning from the direction of Ulithi, was ordered to complete fuelling and join the others. By midnight, the three carrier task groups, with Halsey himself in *New Jersey* and Lee in *Washington*, and all their attendant battleships, cruisers and destroyers, were steaming north at 16 knots. Bogan and Lee both signalled their misgivings but were ignored. Sixty-five ships were on their way to engage Ozawa's remaining seventeen. Not one ship, not even a destroyer, was left to guard the San Bernardino.

This was bad enough, but worse was to follow. At Leyte, the misunderstandings inherent in a divided command—with Halsey responsible to Nimitz and Kinkaid to MacArthur—were compounded by delays, mistakes and faults in communications. At 3.12 p.m. Halsey had signalled to his ships that he was going to form a Task Force 34 of four battleships, including *New Jersey*, two heavy cruisers, three light cruisers and fourteen destroyers, all drawn from Davison's and Bogan's groups, commanded by Lee, which would 'engage decisively at long ranges' whilst the carriers kept clear. King and Nimitz were information addressees of this signal, and Kinkaid's staff intercepted it and showed it to him.

So, when Halsey signalled at 8.24 p.m. that he was proceeding north with three groups 'to attack enemy carrier force at dawn', King, Nimitz and Kinkaid were all reassured that the powerful

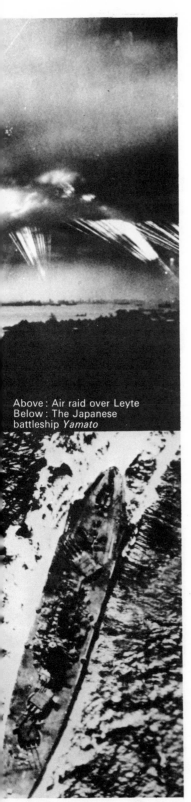

Above: Air raid over Leyte
Below: The Japanese
battleship *Yamato*

surface force had been formed and left on guard. None of them dreamed that Halsey's TF 34 remained an intention and not an action. Even Mitscher, when woken and asked his opinion, said he was sure Halsey had the situation under control, and went back to sleep.

Had a supreme commander been appointed for the Pacific, such a succession of misunderstandings would have been inconceivable. But, as it was, Kurita was able to steam through the night unchallenged, and at 6.46 the next morning, about fifteen minutes after dawn, the lookouts on Admiral Clifton Sprague's carrier *Fanshaw Bay* off Samar reported anti-aircraft fire to the north-westward. A minute later a pilot on anti-submarine patrol some twenty miles to the north reported to a stupefied air operations room in *Fanshaw Bay* that he was being *fired on by a force of battleships, cruisers and destroyers*! Admiral Sprague ordered him to check his identification. But it was no mistake. Soon, the massive pinnacles and turrets of the Japanese capital ships' superstructures could be seen above the northern horizon. At 6.48 the first heavy calibre shells threw up huge splashes close to *Fanshaw Bay's* bows.

The Leyte troop anchorages were guarded by ships of the Seventh Fleet under Kinkaid. Air cover was provided by Task Group 77.4, under Rear-Admiral Thomas Sprague, which had sixteen 'baby flat-top' escort carriers, three of them converted tankers and the rest 'Kaiser-built' on the West Coast. They were deployed in three units, with call signs Taffy 1 (Sprague), Taffy 2 (Rear-Admiral F. B. Stump) and Taffy 3 (Rear-Admiral Clifton F. 'Ziggy' Sprague). Between them they mounted 235 fighters (Wildcats and Hellcats) and 143 Avengers. Their duties were to provide CAPs over the landing beaches and operations immediately inland, strike at airfields in the Visayan Islands, and provide anti-submarine cover for the whole area. The Taffys were not trained for or supposed to attack Japanese heavy ships.

Although 'Ziggy' Sprague had suffered the biggest early morning shock of any admiral in modern times, he did what he could and did it well. He ordered his six carriers to turn eastward into wind, work up to their full speed of 17½ knots and launch every possible aircraft with orders to attack. They were helped by a fortunate rain squall which gave them cover at a crucial period. At the same time he radioed for help. But Oldendorf was far to the south, short of ammunition after his night's exertions. Thomas Sprague's Taffy 1 was 130 miles away, and it was problematical whether his aircraft could reach the scene before the Japanese heavy guns blasted Taffy 3 out of the water.

Thus Ziggy's ships were on their own for the time being and at 7.16 he ordered the destroyers *Hoel*, *Heermann* and *Johnston* to counter-attack. They went in with the utmost gallantry. *Johnston* frustrated an attack by Kurita's own destroyers, exchanged shots with the battleship *Kongo* and put one torpedo in the heavy

149

cruiser *Kumano* before she herself was hit by three 14-inch and three 6-inch shells; as one of *Johnston's* surviving officers said, 'it was like a puppy being smacked by a truck'. *Johnston* was badly damaged and sank at 10.10. *Hoel* attacked *Kongo*, *Yamato* and *Haguro* before she too was hit and sunk.

The destroyers' torpedoes forced *Yamato* out of the battle line at an important moment. Kurita's handling of his ships in general was poor. He had been as surprised by the encounter as Sprague. He and his staff believed that the escort carriers were fleet carriers and the destroyers cruisers. He believed he had run up against the full Task Force 38. He bungled the station-changing from cruising formation to battle line and when he ordered 'General Attack' his ships steamed more or less independently, attacked piecemeal, and invited defeat in detail.

This indeed was what Ziggy Sprague achieved, by sheer persistence. Kurita had overwhelming strength but he seemed always bemused by the ferocity with which his enemy counter-attacked him. Destroyers and destroyer escorts ran in, fired torpedoes and guns and sheered away. While his ships were distracted, aircraft from Taffy 3, assisted now by many from Taffy 1 and 2, attacked with bombs, torpedoes and guns, and when their ammunition was exhausted, returned to make 'dry runs'. Frequent forced alterations prevented Kurita's ships from closing, while Sprague's carriers kept doggedly on, altering now and again to avoid salvoes.

Opposite above: U.S. Avenger torpedo-bomber reconnaissance aircraft over Leyte

Above centre: General MacArthur wading ashore at Leyte

Above: U.S. troops landing stores at Leyte

Left: Action on Leyte—three U.S. infantrymen pinned down by Japanese machine-gun fire during 'mopping up' operations

Leyte Gulf, 25 October 1944.
A kamikaze hit on the U.S.
carrier *St. Lô*

The heavy cruisers *Chikuma*, *Tone*, *Haguro* and *Chokai* scored thirteen 8-inch hits on *Kalinin Bay* but she survived. When the cruisers turned to *Gambier Bay*, they sank her. However, four Avengers from *Kitkun Bay* sank *Chokai* with four torpedoes, and a well-coordinated attack by Wildcats and Avengers from Stump's Taffy 2 sank *Chikuma*. Another heavy cruiser, *Suzuya*, hit in the first air attacks, sank later.

Kurita could still have won a great victory but at 9.11 he broke off the action. He meant merely to re-form his ships and return, but he did not do so. By noon the Battle of Samar was over. Sprague had lost two escort carriers, two destroyers and a destroyer escort (*S. B. Roberts*). He had over a thousand men killed or missing, and nearly another thousand wounded. But he had defeated Kurita.

Land-based suicide aircraft, making one of the first of their ominous appearances, damaged the carriers *Santee* and *Suwannee*. One aircraft plunged through the flight deck of *St Lo* and sank her. But Kurita was also still under air attack and one last bomb

152

hit on *Nagato* seemed to make up his mind. At 12.36 p.m. he signalled Tokyo that he was retiring. The great prize for which so many Japanese men and ships had been sacrificed was lost. The hopes and plans of Toyoda and Ozawa, and of Kurita himself, were brought to nothing. Kurita seems to have been in a mental daze throughout the battle. But he had had his flagship sunk underneath him. He had been under air attack for most of three days. He thought he faced massive air counter-attack from Halsey's carriers and from airfields on shore. He had heard the news of the disaster to Nishimura's Southern Force. As Churchill magnanimously wrote of Kurita, 'those who have endured a similar ordeal may judge him'.

Understandably, as Ziggy Sprague fought off Kurita, the ether thickened with ever more frantic appeals for help. Some, from Kinkaid to Halsey, were not even coded, but in plain language. One, from Nimitz to Halsey, was in even plainer language: 'Where is Task Force 34?' For cryptographic security, every message had 'padding' at its beginning and end. Unfortunately, the encoding officer at Pearl Harbor, possibly influenced by unconscious memories of Balaclava (whose anniversary fell on that date, 25 October) used 'padding' with Tennysonian resonances. In the heat of decoding in *New Jersey* the 'complete' message passed to the flag deck was: 'Where is Task Force 34 the world wonders?' Mortally insulted (the message was repeated to King and Kinkaid), Halsey took off his cap, smashed it to the deck, and jumped on it.

However, the point of the query was still valid. At 4.30 a.m. on 25 October, Mitscher ordered all carriers to prepare a full deck load for a strike at first light. The first of six strikes that day reached Ozawa's ships at about 8 a.m. *Zuikaku*, the last surviving villain of Pearl Harbor, *Zuiho*, *Chitose* and one destroyer were sunk, and another carrier, *Chiyoda*, abandoned (to be sunk by U.S. cruisers next day). It was yet another victory, but weight for weight, and plane for plane, TF 38's had not done as well as Spruance's aircraft at Midway or even Ziggy Sprague's earlier that morning. Having received Nimitz's 'Task Force 34' signal, Halsey detached most of Lee's TF 34, including *New Jersey*, with Bogan's carrier group and sent them south to help Kinkaid. But they were too late by several hours to intercept Kurita, who was long gone through the San Bernardino Strait by the time they arrived. Ozawa's ships had been only 42 miles away from *New Jersey's* guns when Halsey broke off. As Halsey said sadly, 'I turned my back on the opportunity I had dreamed of since my days as a cadet.'[20]

The Japanese had lost a fleet carrier, three light fleet carriers, three battleships, six heavy cruisers, four light cruisers, nine destroyers and a submarine. Against that, the U.S. Navy had lost a light fleet carrier, two escort carriers, two destroyers, a destroyer escort and a submarine.

THE SUBMARII
WAR

'Press home all attacks,' wrote Rear-Admiral James Fife U.S.N., Commander Submarines Southwest Pacific, in his standing orders. 'Pursue relentlessly, remembering that the mission is to destroy every possible enemy ship. Do not let cripples escape or leave them to sink—make sure that they do sink.'

The American submariners in the Pacific, very ably assisted by the British and the Dutch, put Admiral Fife's orders faithfully into effect and achieved devastating results. By VJ-Day, August 1945, Allied submarines in the Far East were actually running out of targets to sink. By that time, although submarines still constituted only 2 per cent of the American effort in the Pacific, American submarines had sunk two-thirds of the total Japanese merchant ship tonnage sunk during the war and had also sunk one out of every three of the Japanese warships sunk. After the war, Tojo himself admitted that there were three main factors which had defeated Japan: the 'leap-frogging' techniques of advance, the strikes by the fast carrier task forces, and the steady attrition of shipping caused by submarines.

The United States and Japanese navies were roughly equal in submarine strength in the Pacific at the outset of the war. Neither navy had had any operational experience of submarines in the First World War. Both had prepared for submarine warfare on a long-range scale, and primarily for use against an enemy's warships. The crucial differences in the Second World War lay in the United States Navy's technological advance, its readiness to profit by tactical experience, and its proper strategic deployment of its submarines. In all three areas the Americans were superior.

At the time of Pearl Harbor, the U.S. Navy had some fifty-five submarines in the Pacific, about half of them at Pearl and the rest with the Asiatic Fleet in the Philippines. Some of the boats belonged to the older and smaller S-Class of 800 to 1,100 tons, but the standard *Gato* Class fleet-type submarine, which carried the heat and burden of the day in Pacific submarine warfare, was an excellent long-range weapon, of some 1,500 tons, with a crew of seven officers and seventy men, a cruising range of 10,000 miles, stores for sixty-day patrols, a surface speed under diesel-electric propulsion of just over 20 knots and a maximum submerged speed on main batteries of 9 knots. The submerged endurance on batteries was 48 hours at $2\frac{1}{2}$ knots. These submarines were armed with eight to ten 21-inch torpedoes, with eighteen reloads, a 3-inch and, later, 5-inch gun on deck and various outfits of .50 calibre anti-aircraft guns.

The Japanese had sixty submarines, forty-seven of the fleet-type I-Class and thirteen of the smaller RO-Class. The I-Class were of some 2,000 tons, with a surface speed of 24 knots and submerged speed of 8 knots, and a cruising range of 10,000 to 17,500 miles. They were armed with twenty-four 21-inch torpedoes in six to eight tubes, with eighteen reloads. They also had one or two deck guns of 4.7- to 5.5-inch, with several AA guns.

155

The one advantage the Japanese submarines had was the quality of their torpedoes. Their 40-knot, oxygen-powered, longer ranged torpedoes had twice the explosive charge of the Americans' and were formidable weapons. American torpedoes were frequently defective and, incredibly, it was nearly two years before the U.S. Navy established the cause of the defects and remedied them. Pre-war, the Navy had been extremely niggardly with torpedoes for practice: to lose a torpedo after a run was a very serious disciplinary offence. The torpedoes nearly always ran eight to ten feet below their proper depth, so that the magnetic detonators, designed to be activated by the target's metal hull, failed to work properly. Similarly, the contact detonators only worked best after an oblique impact, thus, ironically, penalizing the very submarine captains who aimed best and hit their targets broadside on. Design faults were compounded by bureaucratic obstruction; shore-bound officers and bureaucrats refused to believe submarine captains who said they had *heard* their torpedoes hitting the target and failing to explode.

For the first months of the war, Japanese submarines had considerable success in sinking Allied warships, especially in the waters of 'Torpedo Junction' in the summer of 1942. But the fatal Japanese tendency to indulge in non-profitable peripheral activities soon began to drain away their submarine patrol strength. The Japanese diverted their submarines to carry midget submarines, to no tactical purpose, or to act as communications links, or to wait at a rendezvous to refuel flying-boats, or to carry out unimportant surface bombardments which had no more than nuisance value of Midway, or Canton Island, or Johnston Island, or (in 1942) the coasts of Vancouver and Oregon. The largest Japanese submarines carried aircraft (which required an hour after surfacing to assemble and launch) which they transported thousands of miles for valueless reconnaissance flights. One submarine, I.25, launched her aircraft loaded with incendiaries with the serious intention of setting light to the forests of North America. As the war progressed, more and more Japanese submarines were taken off patrols and used to carry men, ammunition and food to beleaguered Japanese island garrisons bypassed by the Allied advance.

The 'scouting' lines of submarines established by the Japanese at various times in the war accomplished very little. Before Midway, they arrived on station far too late, when the American fleet had long passed them by. Before the Philippine Sea, they were severely mauled by *England* and her consorts. The sixteen Japanese submarines deployed at sea before and around Leyte Gulf sank one ship, a destroyer escort. Probably the best strategic use the Japanese could have made of their submarines would have been to make a determined effort to cut the supply lines from Pearl Harbor to Australia and Micronesia. They made no such effort. There was never any submarine war in the Pacific

The giant Japanese submarine aircraft carrier I-400

remotely comparable with the struggle against the Atlantic U-boat. The U.S. Navy began escorting their ships with convoys in the Pacific but by the end of 1943 there was so little enemy submarine activity that single ships were steaming across the Pacific unescorted.

The Allies, too, used submarines for a great variety of purposes in the Far East: to land and take off secret agents, saboteurs, political V.I.P.s, coast-watchers, refugees and commando parties; to carry out air-sea rescue, weather reporting, and photo-reconnaissance of beaches and shorelines; to act as radar picket ships, radio beacons, and navigational marker buoys for ships and landing craft on their way in to an assault beach; to locate enemy minefields by sonar; to carry stores and aviation fuel (as at Guadalcanal); and to carry out shore bombardments with guns or rockets. Where a target was too small to warrant a torpedo, submarines in inshore waters sent boarding parties to lay demolition charges, or sank the targets by gunfire.

But these multifarious duties were kept firmly subsidiary to the main purpose of carrying out offensive patrols against enemy warships and merchant ships. In 1942 American submarines were equipped with excellent SD air search and SJ surface warning radar sets, and began to carry out night attacks by radar. Japanese submarines and escort vessels were not fitted with radar until much later in the war and survivors of Japanese anti-submarine forces complained after the war that they were like blind men trying to fight the sighted.

To misuse of submarines in exotic sideshows, the Japanese Navy added an almost complete failure to safeguard their own surface ships against submarines. The Japanese were obsessed with the idea of an offensive war. Like the British in the First World War, they regarded convoys as 'defensive' and therefore somehow demeaning and unworthy of a warrior nation. They did not introduce escorts until late in 1943, and even then they never approached the standard of the highly-drilled escort groups of the Atlantic. At the same time, the Japanese planned to build twenty more aircraft carriers, designed for the offensive, and began to convert the third *Yamato* Class hull into a giant aircraft carrier, the 60,000-ton *Shinano*. With the personnel and materials involved in these projects, they could have built scores of invaluable escort vessels.

The Japanese came nowhere near matching American technological invention. Submarine warfare is a subtle weapon which needs constant fine tuning. The Japanese ended the war with the same anti-submarine weapons with which they began it, a somewhat inaccurate depth-charge and a haphazardly aimed air bomb. They made no proper assessment of submarine actions and really had no way of knowing for certain whether they had sunk a submarine or not. They optimistically assumed that they had sunk a submarine every time they attacked one.

The Pacific Submarine Force began 1943 with fifty-three submarines and, despite the lack of an efficient torpedo until late in the year, they sank twenty-two Japanese warships and 296 merchant ships for a total tonnage of 1,335,240 tons sunk. Running from Pearl Harbor, Fremantle and Brisbane, the operational patrol range of the submarines was enormous, from the Aleutians and Kuriles, where the antiquated pre-war S-boats were normally stationed, to the coasts of Malaya and Burma (*Grenadier* was lost in the Indian Ocean, off the west coast of Thailand, in April 1943). Radar-assisted attacks became commonplace, and co-ordinated attack group tactics were introduced, using 'wolf-packs' of three or four submarines operating together to detect, follow and attack targets. The Japanese belatedly introduced convoys in November 1943, but their escorts were poorly organized and they never at any time managed to achieve co-operation between the Army and the Navy over long-range land-based aircraft cover for convoys; the Japanese never had any equivalent of the patrolling Liberator or Catalina armed with depth-charges. All the same, the Japanese still contrived to sink fifteen American submarines during the year with the loss of 1,129 officers and men. The Japanese lost twenty-seven submarines from all causes.

For the Pacific submarine, 1944 was the big year. The year began with seventy-five submarines, nearly all of them fleet boats, the old S-Class having been relegated to training duties, and plenty of targets: the figures of tonnage sunk soared, to 545 ships, of 2,140,000 tons, nearly a third of the ships being tankers. Submarines sank seven Japanese tankers in January, the carrier strike on Truk sank another five of over 50,000 tons on 17 February, and two days later Commander Dykes in *Jack* sank four tankers of 20,000 tons from a convoy of five, in an all-day action in the South China Sea.

In April, Admiral King ordered submarines to make Japanese destroyers their second priority targets, after capital ships, but before tankers and freighters. The submarine captains hardly needed urging to retaliate against their old enemies. By the end of the war, submarines had sunk thirty-nine Japanese destroyers, one of the most successful captains being Commander Sam Dealey in *Harder*, who sank three destroyers in three days off Tawitawi early in June, having already sunk one in April, off the Marianas. Dealey won the Congressional Medal of Honor, but he and *Harder* were lost off Luzon in August, on their sixth war patrol.

After the Battle of the Philippine Sea more submarines were released to operate against merchant shipping, and in August the Pacific submarine base moved to Saipan, 3,500 miles nearer the action than Pearl Harbor. Japanese convoys became even smaller and were forced to leave their coastal route up the west side of Luzon and hug the eastern coast of China instead. The wide stretch of the East China Sea from Luzon Strait across to Formosa and the Chinese coast was nicknamed 'Convoy College'.

Group tactics had been refined and wolf-packs had picturesque names, based on their senior officer's surname or nationality, such as 'Blair's Blasters', 'the Mickey Finns', 'Wogan's Wolves', 'Coye's Coyotes' and 'Clarey's Crushers'.

Individual submarine 'aces' were beginning to appear. Commander 'Red' Ramage, commanding *Parche* in a wolf-pack with *Steelhead* and *Hammerhead*, attacked a Japanese convoy in the Luzon Strait on 30/31 July and sank a tanker, two transports and two passenger-cargo ships, for a total of 39,000 tons. Another pack, of *Picuda*, *Redfish* and *Spadefish*, under Commander G. R. Donaho, sank four ships out of one convoy and finished their patrols with a total of 64,456 tons sunk. In *Tang*, off Formosa, on 23 October, Commander Richard O'Kane sank three heavily laden ships out of four, and followed them with a tanker on the 24th. Returning for another attack, *Tang* was hit by one of her own torpedoes running amuck. O'Kane, and three survivors from on deck, were later joined by another eight who had made a successful escape from the flooded submarine, on the bottom 160 feet below. All were captured, and survived the war.

In October, sixty-eight submarines sank 320,906 tons of Japanese shipping, the highest monthly total of the war. In November, they sank another 214,506 tons. By then, targets were already getting noticeably fewer, but on the 29th *Archerfish*, commanded by Commander Joe Enwright, pulled off the biggest coup of any submarine in the war. *Archerfish* was on lifeguard patrol for B-29s, on station about a hundred miles south of Tokyo Bay when, just before 9 p.m. on the 28th, she obtained a radar contact. It was identified as a large ship, travelling fast and zigzagging. It was in fact an aircraft carrier, making about 20 knots, escorted by three or four destroyers. Enwright surfaced and set off as hard as he could go, to gain a firing position ahead of the target, signalling to Pearl Harbor the action he was taking. Although *Archerfish* was going at full speed, encouraged by a reply from Admiral Charles Lockwood, ComSubPac, 'Keep after him Joe, your picture is on the piano!', it seemed that the target would get away. But at 3 a.m. on the 29th the position was radically changed when the carrier altered to the south and Enwright found himself directly in his target's path. He dived for the attack and fired a salvo of six torpedoes at 1,400 yards range. Two hits were heard, followed by four more, and then what were thought to be 'breaking-up' noises. There were also about a dozen depth-charges, which did *Archerfish* no damage. When Enwright cautiously looked through his periscope at 6 a.m., he could see nothing. Whatever it was had gone, or sunk.

Enwright knew his target was big, but she was in fact the 60,000-ton super-carrier *Shinano*, the largest carrier in the world at that time. She had been four years in the building but only ten days in commission. She had left Tokyo Bay for her maiden voyage at 6 p.m., on passage for the Inland Sea, where it was judged safer from air attacks, for her final fitting-out. She was formidably strong, with armoured sides and over two feet of concrete under her steel flight deck. She was thought invulnerable to bombing attacks, and was also considered invulnerable to *Archerfish*'s six torpedoes. So she should have been. But her 1,900 crew had never been to sea in her before and had never trained as a ship's company. Many of her pumps were not fitted or not connected up. Piping was missing or incomplete. Her doors were not watertight and her bulkheads had hundreds of holes in them. Human bucket chains were formed but they were soon discouraged and melted away. Flooding spread. Orders were disregarded. Discipline began to break down. Men began to assemble on the flight deck, waiting for the end, which came just before 11 a.m., when *Shinano* capsized to starboard, rolled over and sank, taking many of her crew with her. She had been in the open sea for less than twenty hours, and had probably the shortest seagoing career of any major warship ever.

The year of 1944 ended with two sharp pieces of shooting by *Redfish* (Commander L. D. McGregor), who scored two hits on the carrier *Junyo* west of Kyushu on 9 December, putting her out of the war, and sank the new 17,500-ton carrier *Unryu* in two attacks on the 19th. Fifteen U.S. submarines had been lost in the Far East that year (with two British submarines, *Stonehenge* and *Stratagem*, lost in the Malacca Strait) but the Japanese lost fifty-four of their U-boats, from all causes, in the same period.

By the spring of 1945 there was only one stretch of water where Japanese ships could still move free of submarine attack—the Sea of Japan itself. In June, even this last resort was penetrated, in Operation BARNEY, when 'Hydeman's Hellcats', a wolf-pack of nine submarines led by Commander E. T. Hydeman in *Sea Dog*, passed through the Tsushima Straits on the night of 6/7 June and, in eleven days, sank twenty-seven merchant ships and the submarine I.122, for a total of 57,000 tons. From then on targets dwindled so much that many more submarines were devoted to life-saving than ship-sinking. In lifeguard patrols for ditched aircrews, submarines had saved 224 men by December 1944. But in eight months of 1945, eighty-six submarines picked up 380 aviators, mostly B-29 crews.

In 1943 the Royal and Dutch navies' submarine strength in the Indian Ocean shrank almost to nothing, but with the defeat of Italy and the disablement of the battleship *Tirpitz* by midget submarines late in 1943, many more boats became available for the Far East. Numbers built up rapidly in 1944 and British and Dutch submarines, running from Trincomalee, carried out patrols all along the western edge of the Malay barrier. One depot ship, *Maidstone*, and a squadron of submarines reached Fremantle in September 1944 and began to operate with the U.S. submarines in the South-west Pacific Area, moving up to the new submarine base in the Philippines at Subic Bay in May.

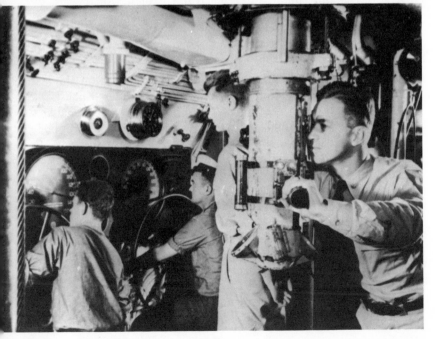

Above: The U.S. submarine
Archerfish

Far left: The officer of the deck
scans the horizon from the
conning tower of the U.S.
submarine *Batfish*

Left: A U.S. submarine
commander at the periscope

The British submarines, too, found targets mostly small, few and far between in the latter months of the war. But on 8 June *Trenchant* (Commander A. R. Hezlet R.N.), patrolling in the mined and restricted waters of the Banka Strait off Sumatra, attacked and sank the heavy cruiser *Ashigara*, returning from Batavia to Singapore with troops on board, with five hits out of a salvo of eight torpedoes in a brilliant attack made from an awkward angle.

In April 1945 a submarine depot ship of an unusual kind reached Pearl Harbor. She was H.M.S. *Bonaventure*, with six XE-craft on board, improved versions of the midget submarines which had attacked *Tirpitz*. There was some American reluctance to use these weapons, which probably stemmed from differences of national temperament: while the British were used to 'messing about in small boats' and had a long history of 'cutting-out' expeditions against fortified enemy harbours, the Americans were either indifferent or hostile to such methods. Also, it may be ungenerous but is probably true to say that some startling exploit of British arms in a wholly American theatre of the war might have 'wiped the eye' of the American publicity machine.

However, approval was obtained and by July 1945 *Bonaventure* and her flock had moved up to Brunei Bay, and from there launched two XE-craft, towed to the scene by orthodox submarines, to attack the heavy cruisers *Myoko* and *Takao*, lying in Singapore roads. *Takao*, already damaged at Leyte, was even further damaged by XE-3's attack, for which her C.O., Lieutenant I. Fraser R.N.R., and his diver, Leading Seaman J. Magennis, both received the Victoria Cross. XE-craft also carried out operations against underwater telegraph cables, which were by that stage of the war the only secure means of Japanese communications. Cables were successfully cut at Cap St Jacques, off Saigon, but the diver in the Lamma Channel off Hong Kong was foiled by deep mud.

On 29 July the Japanese submarine service had almost the last laugh of the war when I.58 (Lieutenant Commander Mochitsura Hashimoto) attacked the heavy cruiser *Indianapolis*, Spruance's old flagship, about 300 miles north-east of the Philippines. *Indianapolis* had carried top-secret material for the atomic bomb from San Francisco and was then on passage from Guam to Leyte. She was unescorted and not zigzagging when she was hit by two torpedoes at 11.50 p.m. and sank about fifteen minutes later. Between 800 and 850 of her complement of 1,199 men survived the attack, though many were burned or wounded. At daylight they expected to be seen and picked up. But nobody came, through a combination of evil circumstances: garbled radio messages, a failure to receive *Indianapolis*'s own signals, unwillingness of Army search aircraft to interfere in what they imagined was Navy business, neglect to make the proper deductions from Hashimoto's intercepted signal of triumph, and a general assump-

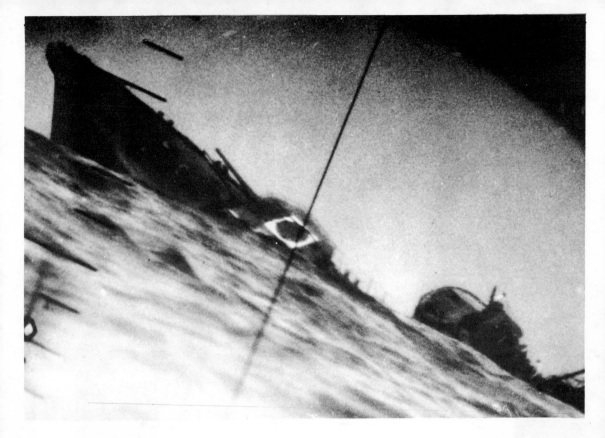

A sinking Japanese destroyer seen through the periscope of the U.S. submarine *Wahoo*

tion that *Indianapolis* had gone somewhere else and was no business of theirs, and that everything was in order. Her absence was not noticed at Leyte, and it was three and a half days before help arrived, at 3.30 p.m. on 2 August. By that time, nearly 500 men had died of thirst, exposure, wounds or shark attack. Only 316 of *Indianapolis*'s people survived. Her captain, Captain C. B. McVay, was censured by the court-martial, and ordered to lose seniority, which was later restored to him. The politicians' handling of the whole affair caused a good deal of resentment in the Navy.

Japan had entered the war in December 1941 with just under six million tons of merchant shipping. By the end of 1942, she had captured or salvaged 670,000 tons and built another 270,000 tons, so that although she had lost 1,123,000 tons, the net loss was only some 177,000 tons. But from then on, Japan's situation deteriorated year by year. In 1943, the gross tonnage lost was 1,800,000, for a net loss of 940,000 tons. In 1944, although Japan had stepped up her building to 1,700,000 tons, her losses were 969 vessels of 3,890,000 tons, with a catastrophic net loss of 2,150,000 tons. In eight months of 1945 she lost another 700 vessels of 1,780,000 tons and at the end of the war had only 1,500,000 tons left, of which only about 500,000 tons was still serviceable. She also had some 1,000,000 tons of wooden shipping, mostly in the Inland Sea. Of these totals, Allied submarines were responsible for sinking 2,200 Japanese merchant vessels and 240 Japanese warships, for a total of 5½ million tons.

11 IWO JIMA & OKINAWA

The suicide aircraft which hit and sank the little escort carrier *St Lo* off Samar on 25 October was one of the earliest signs of an approaching storm. On 15 October, off Luzon, a single Judy bomber piloted by Rear-Admiral Masafumi Arima, in command of the 26th Air Flotilla, crashed with its 500-lb bomb on the flight deck of the carrier *Franklin*, doing little damage but killing three men and wounding twelve. At various times during the war, pilots had deliberately crashed into their targets in the heat of an action. But this was a calculated act of self-immolation, and it was followed by a campaign of such attacks, as though the Japanese were beginning to use land-based aircraft as humanly-guided missiles to substitute for their lack of carriers at sea. The suicide bomber was called the 'Kamikaze', or 'divine wind', recalling an old Japanese legend of the Wind God Ise who on 14 and 15 August 1281 had saved Japan by summoning up a typhoon to disperse a great Sino-Mongol invasion fleet of 3,500 ships assembled by Kublai Khan. In her present extremity, some sort of similar divine intervention would be needed again to save Japan. The kamikazes were therefore a weapon born of desperation. They could not win the war for Japan—but they could compensate for Japan's critical lack of trained aircrew.

The new suicide units were formed by Vice-Admiral Takajiro Onishi, who arrived in Luzon to take over command of the 1st Air Fleet on 17 October. The first pilots were volunteers of the 201st Air Group and were led on their first organized sortie by Lieutenant Yukio Seti. The heavy cruiser H.M.A.S. *Australia* was hit on 21 October; *St Lo* and her sister carrier suffered a much heavier attack on the 25th. From then on during the landings at Mindoro in December and at Lingayen Gulf in January hardly a day passed without kamikaze sorties by groups of half dozen aircraft or single planes.

Out to sea, the Wind God Ise once again tried to assist Japan. On 18 December TF 38 ran into the full fury of a tropical typhoon. Three destroyers capsized and sank, seven other ships were badly damaged, 186 aircraft blown overboard or irreparably damaged and nearly 800 officers and men killed. It was, as Nimitz said, the Navy's greatest loss without any compensating return, since Savo Island. A court of inquiry blamed the losses on a failure to take seamanlike precautions, and placed the blame squarely on Halsey.

TF 38 might have experienced the fury of the weather, but they escaped the violence of the enemy, preventing losses to the kamikazes by doubling up the proportion of fighters to bombers embarked, carrying out ferocious and continued strafing sweeps over airfields and by setting outlying destroyers as radar pickets. All incoming aircraft had to make a circuit round the pickets whilst they were 'vetted', by radar and visually. Any intruders hoping to follow TF 38's own aircraft back to the task force were then 'weeded out' and shot down by the picket CAPs.

Opposite: Okinawa. A Marine looks over the rubble of Naha, the capital of Okinawa

To support the Lingayen Gulf landings, Halsey took TF 38
eastwards into the South China Sea, where major U.S. warships
had not operated since 1942. TF 38's aircraft struck at targets in
Formosa, Hong Kong and Hainan, ranging freely over Japanese
possessions as far north as Amoy and Swatow. It was a well
planned and well executed sortie, showing that Halsey could
now operate in Far Eastern waters with a freedom nobody had
had since Nagumo three years earlier.

By mid January Japanese air power in Luzon had been
virtually extinguished. Admiral Fukudome took the survivors
northwards to Formosa, leaving individual aircraft to make their
own best way to safety. However, by the end of January kamikazes from the Philippines had flown 421 sorties, and had lost
378 of their number. But they had sunk sixteen ships, including
another escort carrier, *Ommanney Bay*, and had damaged eighty-
seven other ships, including twenty-two carriers, five battleships,
ten cruisers and twenty-eight destroyers or destroyer escorts.

At first, Halsey and the men of his fleet simply could not grasp
the true nature of their new opponents. To Western minds there
was something immeasurably repellent in this horrifying self-
sacrifice. As Halsey himself wrote, after the war, 'I think that
most of us took it as a sort of token terror, a tissue-paper dragon.
The psychology behind it was too alien to ours: Americans, who
fight to live, find it hard to realise that other people will fight to
die. We could not believe that even the Japanese, for all their
hara-kiri tradition, could muster enough recruits to make such a
corps really effective. We were violently disillusioned the very
next day. They missed the *Enterprise*, in Davison's group, but they

hit two of his other carriers, the *Franklin* and the *Belleau Wood*, killing a total of 158 men, destroying 45 planes, and requiring the withdrawal of both ships for repairs.'[21] The kamikaze wind was to blow more strongly for some months to come, while the Allied view of it turned from incredulity to disgust. The sinister implications of the suicide aircraft, its unpredictability, the manner in which it could turn and come again after it had apparently passed the ship, made it the one weapon which came nearest to affecting the fighting morale of the Allied Navy's bluejackets, especially those in exposed upperdeck positions. But, incredibly, most of the kamikaze pilots were indeed volunteers and post-war interrogation of the survivors confirmed their defiant pride in their chosen corps.

The Third Fleet returned to Ulithi for rest and recreation on 25 January. It was high time for a break. The fleet had been at sea continuously except for short periods for the previous eighty-four days. They claimed to have destroyed over 7,000 Japanese aircraft, sunk over ninety Japanese warships of various kinds, and nearly 600 merchant ships of over a million tons. While the bluejackets of the fleet relaxed, swam and drank beer, Spruance relieved Halsey, the fleet once more becoming the Fifth Fleet and the Fast Carrier Task Force TF 58 again. Halsey left with a generous signal of praise and thanks to his men. Although somewhat unpredictable (and some of his own staff thought the handling of such a huge fleet was too much for Halsey), Halsey was always as ready to take the blame as to hand out praise. He was much loved, and had become a national hero back in the States.

With the cooler, more calculating mind of Spruance now in charge, the great fleet addressed itself to the task of taking the island of Iwo Jima. While Kinkaid's Seventh Fleet ships went south with MacArthur's South-west Pacific Area force to attack islands in the southern Philippines and, ultimately, in Borneo (minus some Fifth Fleet ships which had been gently and tactfully disentangled by Nimitz, now based at Guam, who needed them for Iwo and Okinawa), the Fifth Fleet sailed from Ulithi on 10 February for a series of strikes against the Japanese mainland— the first since General Doolittle, what seemed several centuries earlier.

Iwo Jima could have been taken unopposed in September 1944. Even in January 1945 the task would not have been so difficult. But the Japanese resistance in the Philippines was so fierce (Yamashita, the army commander, and the remaining 50,000 of his troops on Luzon did not surrender until 15 August) that the assault on Iwo Jima could not be launched until 19 February. By that time the island commander, Lieutenant-General Tadamichi Kuribayashi, had made Iwo into a really formidable fortress, in which the natural qualities of the terrain were brilliantly allied to the fanatical resistance of the Japanese garrison.

Iwo Jima was subjected to the heaviest, most prolonged and, ultimately, least effective air and naval bombardment of any Pacific island. It began with bombing raids in August 1944, continued in September, October and December. Heavy cruisers bombarded late in December and early in January. The nearby islands of Chichi and Haha Jima were also pounded to prevent reinforcements being staged through them. Iwo Jima was bombed day and night for two weeks from 31 January. By D-Day an estimated 6,800 tons of bombs and 22,000 rounds of shell from 16-inch to 5-inch had landed on the island.

Unfortunately, it was largely to no avail. As 'Howling Mad' Smith said when he first saw Iwo, 'this is our toughest yet'. The labyrinth of artillery, mortar and machine-gun positions, connected by underground tunnels and passages, could not be neutralized by bombardment, no matter how heavy. They were virtually impossible to spot, and were only revealed when a direct hit physically blew away the volcanic sand of the island and the protective camouflage erected by the Japanese.

The struggle for Iwo Jima between the U.S. Marines and the defending Japanese has become one of the legends of the Second World War. The Marines had to take the island literally yard by yard. As Iwo was only 4½ miles long by 2½ wide at its widest point,

the Marines could be assisted at every point by some of the most intense, sustained and accurate naval bombardment support of the war.

The kamikazes made only one intervention, on 21 February, when thirty-two aircraft from Katori in Japan refuelled at Hachijo Jima and attacked the fleet. They penetrated the screen, hit and sank the escort carrier *Bismarck Sea* and damaged five other ships including the carrier *Saratoga*. Otherwise, as Kuribayashi well knew, Iwo Jima was sealed off from all reinforcement. But, husbanding and deploying his garrison with supreme skill, Kuribayashi inflicted on the U.S. Marines and Navy casualties of 5,931 men killed or died of wounds, and another 17,272 wounded. Of his own garrison of 22,000 men, only 216 were taken prisoner. Kuribayashi himself was not one of them.

The airfields on the island were at once taken in hand by the Seabees and by the end of the war some 2,400 B-29 landings had been made there, with many more long-range fighter sorties by Mustangs, who would not otherwise have had the range to accompany the B-29s to Japan. But Iwo's main use was perhaps as an emergency landing field for B-29s which otherwise would probably have been lost. As one B-29 pilot said, 'Whenever I land on this island, I thank God and the men who fought for it.'

The flight deck of the U.S. carrier *Saratoga* after a kamikaze hit off Iwo Jima

Above: U.S. Marines dig in on Motoyama airfield no. 1, Iwo Jima. Mount Suribachi is in the background

Above centre: U.S. Marines of the 5th Division work their way up the slope from Red Beach One towards Mount Suribachi

Above right: Devil's breath on hell's island—two Marines hit the deck to throw a scorching inferno at a Japanese strongpoint on Iwo Jima

Left : Marine rocket trucks on
Iwo Jima

171

The U.S. carrier *Franklin* burning after a bombing attack, March 1945

The first Seabees landed on Iwo on D-Day and they began work on No. 1 Motoyama airstrip within five days. By 20 April there were 7,600 Seabees on the island. These remarkable men of the U.S. Navy Construction Battalions (CBs, or Seabees) were responsible for the vital work of clearing wreckage from captured islands, and constructing airstrips, harbour facilities and buildings and bridges of all kinds. Most of them had had experience of the construction industry in civilian life, but nothing in their previous existences could have prepared them for the pace of the Pacific War. The Seabees always worked against time, often starting work under enemy fire, as at Henderson, and alternately driving bulldozers and beating off enemy counter-attacks, as, for instance, at Momote airfield on Los Negros in the Admiralty Islands. Such was the speed at which they worked that within a few weeks of the capture of the Marianas the five airfields on Guam, Saipan and Tinian were together capable of operating 180 Superfortresses.

Iwo Jima was declared secured on 16 March (although, surprisingly, as many as 867 more Japanese surrendered in April and May, and isolated parties held out even longer). By that date, the battle had moved to Okinawa, the largest island in the Ryukyus, only 350 miles from metropolitan Japan. TF 58 began the strategic isolation of Okinawa with strikes at airfields in Kyushu and Honshu, and at shipping in the Inland Sea, on 18 and 19 March. The Japanese retaliated with more suicide attacks. *Enterprise*, *Yorktown* and *Wasp* were all hit, and *Franklin*, hit for the third time, was very badly damaged, with nearly 800 of her company being killed. Thanks to superb firefighting and damage control, *Franklin* survived and reached the United States.

The Ryukyus had been closed to outsiders for many years before the war and accurate intelligence information about Okinawa was scanty. It was believed that the Japanese had about 50,000 troops on the island. In fact, Okinawa was defended by

two divisions and one brigade, some 70,000 men, of the Japanese 32nd Army, under another very able field commander, Lieutenant-General Mitsuru Ushijima. With additional naval and native Okinawan personnel, the total garrison was nearly 100,000 men, mostly concentrated in the southern stronghold of Shuri, the ancient capital of Okinawa.

By March 1945 the Japanese had nearly 6,000 aircraft assigned to the defence of the approaches to Japan, most based in Japan and Formosa, and about 4,000 of them kamikazes. The 10th Air Fleet, based in Kyushu, had some 2,000 aircraft, of which 1,300 were in training but were to be ready for combat by 30 April. By the end, the Japanese committed about 10,000 aircraft to the defence of Okinawa. There were four all-weather airfields on Okinawa, at Yontan, Kadena, Machinato and Naha, a fifth building at Yonabaru, and a sixth on the offshore island of Ie Shima.

For the Allies, the task of taking Okinawa was given to the U.S. 10th Army, under Lieutenant-General Simon Bolivar Buckner Jr, who had spent the previous four years organizing the defence of Alaska. The 10th Army was newly formed but its two corps were veterans: the 24th (Major-General John R. Hodge) had captured Leyte, and the 3rd Amphibious Marine Corps (Major-General Roy S. Geiger U.S.M.C.) had taken Guam and Peleliu. Its total strength was some 182,000 men, although more than half a million men were to be engaged on Okinawa before the end. Richmond Kelly Turner was in command of the Joint Expeditionary Force, which sailed from eleven different ports, from Seattle to Ulithi, and from Pearl Harbor to Noumea, in 430 troopships, which were only part of a total invasion fleet of 1,457 ships.

L-Day for the landing was fixed for 1 April, Easter Sunday, and the preliminary air and sea bombardments began during the five previous days of Holy Week. The Japanese struck back with kamikaze attacks, one of which damaged *Indianapolis*, Spruance's flagship, so that he had to shift his flag to the battleship *New Mexico*. This was a foretaste of what was to come.

The Japanese had transferred their 9th Division from Okinawa to Formosa late in· 1944 and did not have enough troops to defend all the outlying islands. On 26 March the 77th Infantry Division landed almost unopposed on the Kerama Retto, a group of small islands fifteen miles west of southern Okinawa. Some 250 suicide motorboats, which comprised most of the Japanese seaborne force in the area, were captured, but more important, the islands made an excellent logistic base, with an anchorage in the immediate operating area. Fleet tenders, oilers and repair ships of Service Squadron 10 had gratefully occupied it within four days. (By contrast, when on 16 April 77th Division landed at Ie Shima, an island which had appeared deserted, not responding to any kind of stimuli by air or sea, they had to kill over 3,000 concealed Japanese before securing the airfield.)

At 4.06 a.m. on the 1st, Turner gave the traditional order 'Land the landing force'. The landings at Hagushi beaches went off marvellously well, much more easily than expected. The only

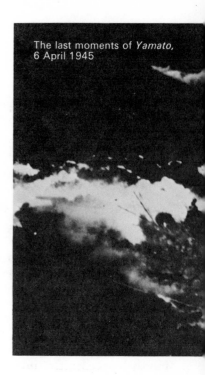

The last moments of *Yamato*, 6 April 1945

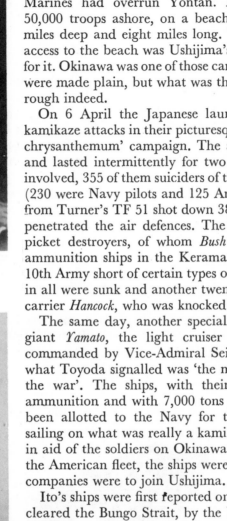

token opposition was from scattered special units left in the area. Ushijima had decided to conserve his strength and engage his enemy inland, where they would not have naval gunfire support. The first assault waves touched down at 8.30 and by ten o'clock units of 24th Corps had taken Kadena airfield. By 1 p.m. the Marines had overrun Yontan. At nightfall 10th Army had 50,000 troops ashore, on a beach-head between two and three miles deep and eight miles long. To allow his enemy such easy access to the beach was Ushijima's error, but he was to make up for it. Okinawa was one of those campaigns where the rough places were made plain, but what was thought to be plain became very rough indeed.

On 6 April the Japanese launched the first of ten massed kamikaze attacks in their picturesquely-named *Kikusui* or 'floating chrysanthemum' campaign. The attacks began at about 3 p.m. and lasted intermittently for two days. Some 660 aircraft were involved, 355 of them suiciders of the *tokko tai* 'special attack' force (230 were Navy pilots and 125 Army). Fighters from TF 58 and from Turner's TF 51 shot down 380 but sheer weight of numbers penetrated the air defences. The main blows fell on the radar picket destroyers, of whom *Bush* and *Calhoun* were sunk. Two ammunition ships in the Kerama Retto were also sunk, leaving 10th Army short of certain types of mortar ammunition. Six ships in all were sunk and another twenty-one damaged, including the carrier *Hancock*, who was knocked out of the battle-line.

The same day, another special attack force, consisting of the giant *Yamato*, the light cruiser *Yahagi* and eight destroyers, commanded by Vice-Admiral Seiichi Ito, sailed from Japan on what Toyoda signalled was 'the most tragic and heroic attack of the war'. The ships, with their magazines crammed full of ammunition and with 7,000 tons of fuel embarked, all that had been allotted to the Navy for the defence of Okinawa, were sailing on what was really a kamikaze sortie on a Homeric scale, in aid of the soldiers on Okinawa. After firing their last shells at the American fleet, the ships were to be beached and their ship's companies were to join Ushijima.

Ito's ships were first reported on the evening of the 6th, as they cleared the Bungo Strait, by the U.S. submarines *Hackleback* and *Threadfin*, patrolling off the east coast of Kyushu. They were sighted again by an aircraft from *Essex* on the morning of the 7th, south-west of Kyushu. Although Turner's battleships moved out to prevent *Yamato* reaching the landing beaches, they would have been outranged by the giant. But in any case, TF 58's aircrews were not to be denied such a target. Between 10 and 10.30 three massive strikes of more than 380 torpedo- and dive-bombers were launched from a position off the Amami Gunto some 250 miles south-east of *Yamato*. The first attack developed just after 12.30. The Japanese had chosen to send all their aircraft to attack the American fleet and *Yamato* had no air cover. Her predicament

Air battle off Ie Shima

The crew of a 'Betty' bomber on an airfield in Japan. The bomber has an Ohka (Cherry Blossom) piloted bomb slung below it

oddly resembled that of *Prince of Wales* and *Repulse*, years before. Admiral Yamamoto, when asked how aircraft could possibly sink huge battleships, had replied 'with torpedo-bombers. The fiercest serpent can be overcome by a swarm of ants.'[22] And so it proved. *Yamato*, one of the most beautiful battleships ever built, whose very name was an ancient and sacred one for Japan herself, sank at 2.23 p.m., after five bomb and ten torpedo hits. With her went Admiral Ito and all but 269 of her company of 2,400 men. *Yahagi* and four of the accompanying destroyers were also sunk. The four remaining destroyers, two badly damaged, returned to Japan. This Battle of the East China Sea was the Imperial Japanese Navy's last spasm of activity at sea.

The next *Kikusui* attack of 185 aircraft on 12/13 April included a new weapon, the Ohka, or Cherry Blossom, which was a small single-seated wooden aircraft, rocket-powered, in effect a piloted 4,000-lb bomb. It was carried to its target area under the belly of a parent bomber and released to plunge towards its target, blasting itself earthwards with its three rockets. The Allies called it *Baka* (foolish) but, with its range of twenty miles from 20,000 feet, it sank one destroyer, *Mannert L. Abele*, and damaged several other ships. Although the *kikusuis* suffered terrible losses, of between 60 and 90 per cent of the aircraft taking part, so that successive waves contained less and less aircraft, they continued to batter the ships off Okinawa. In spite of the radar pickets' warnings, doubled and redoubled anti-aircraft armament, extensive use of close-proximity shell fuses, and ever more skilful and devoted fighter opposition, the Divine Wind, as the Americans said, kept on coming. The radar picket destroyer *Laffey* was

attacked twenty-two times in eighty minutes, suffered six kamikaze and four bomb hits, one kamikaze and one bomb near-miss and prolonged strafing. But she survived and made it to Guam, with over 100 casualties. Kamikazes hit *New Mexico*, *Maryland* and *Tennessee*, the carriers *Bunker Hill*, *Enterprise* and *Intrepid* (again), and a long list of minor warships and landing craft. By mid May TF 58 had to be reorganized in three groups because there were no longer enough carriers for four.

There was an element of personal threat in the suicide attack which had been absent from naval warfare since the days of boarding and hand-to-hand fighting. All eye-witnesses were convinced that the suicider was aiming for them, personally. All the dramatic intensity, the spectacular action, the fanaticism and the trial of human courage, of the sea war against Japan are contained in the description of one kamikaze attack on *Enterprise* on 13 May 1945:

> This pilot knew his job thoroughly and all those who watched him make his approach felt their mouths go dry. In less than a minute he would have attained his goal: there could be little doubt that this was to crash his machine on the deck of the *Enterprise*. All the batteries were firing: the five-inch guns, the 40-mm and the 20-mm, even the rifles. The Japanese aircraft dived through a rain of steel. It had been hit in several places and seemed to be trailing a banner of flame and smoke, but it came on, clearly visible, hardly moving, the line of its wings as straight as a sword.
>
> The deck was deserted; every man, with the exception of the gunners, was lying flat on his face. Flaming and roaring, the fireball passed in front of the 'island' superstructure and crashed with a terrible impact just behind the for'ard lift. The entire vessel was shaken, some forty yards of the flight deck folded up like a banana-skin: an enormous piece of the lift, at least a third of the platform, was thrown over three hundred feet into the air. The explosion killed fourteen men; those boys would never laugh and joke again. The last earthly impression they took with them was the picture of the kamikaze trailing his banner of flame and increasing in size with lightning rapidity.[23]

South of Okinawa, off the Sakishima Archipelago, the carriers of the Royal Navy were also suffering kamikaze attack. One of the carriers, H.M.S. *Victorious*, had in fact served in the Pacific earlier in the war. In the desperate days of October 1942, after the Battle of Santa Cruz, the U.S. Chiefs of Staff had asked the Admiralty for the loan of one, or better still, two carriers, to operate in the Pacific. The request was received less than rapturously by the Admiralty, who did not at first appreciate the true American predicament and who in any case had many other commitments, principally the 'Torch' landings in North Africa. It was not until December 1942 that *Victorious* could be spared. She reached Pearl Harbor in March 1943, retrained her ship's company and aircrews in American practice and American aircraft, and joined the U.S. fleet in May. She and *Saratoga* operated with Halsey's fleet that summer and took part in the covering operation for the landings of MacArthur's forces in New Georgia, before returning home via the U.S.A. in September 1943.

The reappearance of a British fleet in the Pacific in the spring of 1945 was the outcome of a long period of fierce political and diplomatic in-fighting. For years, Churchill hankered after Operation CULVERIN—the forcing of the Malacca Straits (which was in fact never carried out). The plans of Lord Mountbatten, Supreme Allied Commander in South-east Asia, for CULVERIN and other major amphibious operations in the Indian Ocean were constantly frustrated by lack of sufficient forces, especially of landing craft. The Foreign Office agreed with Churchill that the centre of gravity of British operations in the East should be in the Indian Ocean, and directed towards the recovery of former British possessions. Remote Pacific islands, no matter what their strategic value, meant nothing to the peoples of occupied Burma, Malaya and Indonesia. In other words, the Japanese must not only be defeated, they must be seen to be defeated. The Joint Chiefs of Staff, supported by Admiral King, urged that the British should address themselves to the reconquest of Indonesia, basing their forces on Brunei. But the Admiralty, and Admiral Sir Bruce Fraser, C.-in-C. of the British Pacific Fleet, disagreed and pressed for the main British fleet to be used in the main theatre of operations—in the Pacific. It was this point of view that Churchill put at Quebec in September 1944, when he offered President Roosevelt the British fleet for the Pacific. Roosevelt instantly accepted.

Admiral King, who was no Anglophile, feared that a British fleet would drain away American logistical resources and insisted that the British be 'self-sufficient'. The British organized a fleet train of tankers, store and repair ships which was possibly the most motley collection of vessels ever assembled: all manner of ships, sailing under several different ensigns, manned by men of several different services and nationalities. The performance of the fleet train in the Pacific, although a triumph, of morale over *matériel*, would not have been enough without the magnificent 'can do' spirit of the American authorities, who interpreted 'self-sufficiency' in an astonishingly generous way.

The fleet was formed in November 1944, reached Australia in January 1945, having carried out strikes against oil refineries in Sumatra on passage, and sailed from Manus in the Admiralty Islands in March. Admiral Fraser had his headquarters ashore, in Sydney. The fleet commander at sea was Vice-Admiral Sir Bernard Rawlings, with Rear-Admiral Sir Philip Vian command-

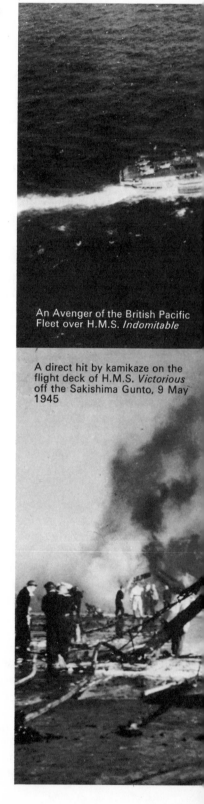

An Avenger of the British Pacific Fleet over H.M.S. *Indomitable*

A direct hit by kamikaze on the flight deck of H.M.S. *Victorious* off the Sakishima Gunto, 9 May 1945

ing the carriers. Although the British Pacific Fleet's initial strength of two battleships, four carriers with 218 aircraft, four cruisers and destroyer escort, was no greater than the average U.S. task group, the fleet was given the designation of a full task force, TF 57.

In the Okinawa campaign, TF 57 was allotted the unglamorous and secondary task of neutralizing by bombing and bombardment the airfields on the Sakishima Gunto, to prevent the Japanese staging reinforcement aircraft through the islands, which ran like a chain of stepping stones from Formosa to Okinawa. Off the Sakishima Gunto, TF 57 stood no chance of glory and every chance of being attacked, and indeed all four carriers suffered kamikaze hits. They were not so heavily armed with AA guns as the American carriers and, in American eyes, 'were not able to look after themselves'. However, they had the advantage of armoured flight-decks which enabled them to operate aircraft within hours (once within ninety minutes) of a kamikaze strike. As one U.S. Navy liaison officer with the British Pacific Fleet put it, 'When a kamikaze hits a U.S. carrier, it's six months' repair in Pearl. In a Limey carrier, it's "Sweepers, man your brooms".'[24]

During May the land battle for Okinawa fell seriously behind schedule. The U.S. Marines had easily secured the northern end of the island in a few days, while in the south, progress was so rapid that the troops began to wonder 'Where is the enemy?' They soon found out, because the further south they pressed, the greater became the Japanese resistance. Ushijima launched two counter-offensives, acting on the true aggressive banzai advice of his Chief of Staff, Lieutenant-General Isamu Cho; both proved futile and abortive, costing many casualties and much of Ushijima's precious remaining artillery. Thereafter, Ushijima relied on the more cautious advice of Colonel Hiromichi Yahara, his senior staff officer (operations) who played the part of a sort of Quintus Fabius Maximus Cunctator of Okinawa most admirably. Yahara advised a policy of attrition, to make the Americans pay for every knob and knoll of territory. The Japanese had to be burned and blasted, with flame-throwers and satchel charges, out of every hole and cave. One position to the east of Shuri, Conical Hill, was taken and retaken several times by the 96th Division before it was finally secured. Yahara's delaying tactics, coupled with heavy rainfall over the whole battle-front, which converted the killing grounds into quagmires, ground General Buckner's offensive almost to a halt. The daily advance dropped to an average of a hundred yards.

The Japanese made intelligent use of mutually supporting defensive positions, with interleaving arcs of fire. Sugar Loaf Hill, west of Shuri, held out for nearly a month because every assault on it was thrown back by supporting fire from adjacent positions which could not themselves be assaulted because of supporting fire from Sugar Loaf. The bloodiest fighting on Okinawa took place on features with 'nursery rhyme' names, such as Sugar Loaf,

Chocolate Drop and Strawberry Hill, an irony not lost on Tokyo Radio, in English language broadcasts to the American troops on Okinawa: 'Sugar Loaf Hill . . . Chocolate Drop . . . Strawberry Hill. Gee, those places sound wonderful! You can just see the candy houses with the white picket fences around them and the candy canes hanging from the trees, their red and white stripes glistening in the sun. But the only thing red about those places is the blood of Americans.'[25]

The stubborn Japanese resistance on land directly affected Allied losses at sea. With not enough airfields on Okinawa to give 10th Army complete air cover, the Allies had to make up the balance from the carriers. TF 58 was therefore forced to stay off-shore, within range of an effective and suicidally inclined shore-based enemy air force, for many weeks. Unlike Colonel Yahara, Mitscher had no desire for a war of attrition; his TF 58 was not designed or intended for this role and he was anxious to get away. When the *kikusui* attacks began to dwindle, Mitscher suggested that land-based air forces, with B-29 raids from the Marianas, could now handle the situation ashore. Spruance, cautious and shrewd as ever, rejected the proposal. It was as well he did, for the kamikazes were by no means finished.

The last *kikusui* waves, the ninth and tenth, of fifty and forty-five aircraft respectively, were launched on 3-7 and 21-22 June. By that time the flying skill of the pilots, never very high, had sunk until many of the kamikaze aircraft were being flown by raw recruits, farm labourers and university students, who could barely hold their machines in the sky, let alone navigate or take evasive action. They were shepherded, 'herded' would perhaps be a better word, by so-called 'Gestapo' aircraft, whose experienced pilots

Opposite: A raid by U.S. carrier aircraft on installations and shipping, Okinawa, 23 March 1945

Below: A U.S. Marine rifleman covers a Japanese soldier emerging from a cave to surrender

directed the kamikazes on to their targets, giving them precise radio instructions (which were intercepted by special 'Y' groups of listeners in Allied ships and gave priceless intelligence of Japanese intentions). The average kamikaze pilot had not the skill to fly very low, or very high, which were the best approaches, and perforce had to fly at a moderate height, and at a steady speed and course, which made him all the easier to chop down out of the sky. Towards the end, when the Japanese were husbanding their aircraft for the attack they knew must come against Japan herself, the kamikazes included many obsolete trainers and slow seaplanes. The main bodies had to conform to their slow speeds, which made them, too, even easier to intercept.

The psychology of the kamikaze pilots remains a mystery to Western minds. They often thought of themselves, and called themselves, robots, but their last letters to their families showed them as anything but that. Yoshi Miyagi was a former student of political economy at Tokyo University, shot down off Okinawa on 19 May. 'The Americans call this suicide,' he wrote.

But this suicide is also a form of sacrifice which can be understood only in Japan, the country of idealism. We, the kamikaze pilots, are nothing more than robots, we can do nothing except remain silent, entreating our compatriots to make Japan into the great country of our dreams. I know that no purpose can any longer be served by my death, but I remain proud of piloting a suicide plane and it is in this state of mind that I die.

Forgive me if my thoughts are disordered. Tomorrow a man in love with liberty will leave this world. I may have given you the impression of being disillusioned, but at the bottom of my heart I am happy to die. I have nothing else to say to you, and I end my letter . . . Yoshi.[26]

By the time Okinawa was declared secured on 21 June, the kamikazes had flown 1,809 sorties and lost 930 aircraft. They sank seventeen ships and damaged 198, including twelve carriers and ten battleships. In all kamikaze operations, the Japanese Navy flew 2,314 sorties and lost 1,228 aircraft. Strangely, they always overestimated the number of ships sunk, and underestimated those damaged. But they actually sank thirty-four ships and damaged the staggering number of 288.

In June Japanese resistance had begun to crumble. Ushijima and Cho committed *seppuku* (ceremonial suicide) together on a cave facing the sea near Mabuni on the south coast, on the evening of the 21st. The wily Yahara survived and became a prisoner of war. Ushijima's army were killed or taken prisoner to the last man, while 10th Army casualties were 7,203 killed or missing (including General Buckner, killed by shell fragments in a forward position on 18 June) and 31,081 wounded. The United States Navy had 4,907 killed or missing, 4,824 wounded; the Royal Navy, 85 killed and missing, 83 wounded.

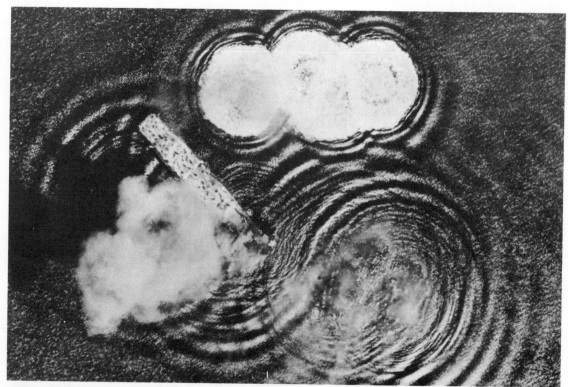

Above: A *Kobe*-class carrier under attack by British aircraft   Below: After the attack

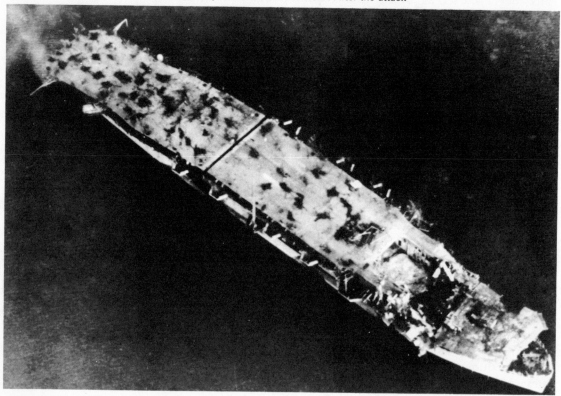

12 VICTORY IN THE PACIFIC

On 27 May Halsey relieved Spruance as fleet commander, while Vice-Admiral McCain relieved Mitscher in command of the carriers, for the final stages of the Okinawa campaign. Almost at once, Halsey was in trouble again with the Wind God Ise. Another typhoon hit part of the Third Fleet on 5 June; one carrier group in particular, manoeuvring to find comfortable courses to steer, contrived to head almost into the eye of the storm. All four of the carriers, *Hornet, Bennington, Belleau Wood* and *San Jacinto*, were damaged, and the heavy cruiser *Pittsburgh* lost 100 feet of her bow. Halsey and McCain were both censured and only Halsey's position as a national hero saved him, once again, from being relieved of his command. And so, it was Halsey, very properly, who was still in command when the Third Fleet sortied out from Leyte on 1 July, 'blood in the eye', to begin the final round of operations (although nobody could have guessed that at the time) in the war at sea against Japan.

By all rational parameters of measurement, Japan was now beaten. But it remained to force her rulers to admit defeat, and it required a colossal weapon, tinged with the awe of the supernatural, to bring that about. In the meantime, the Chiefs of Staff's planners went ahead with plans for Operation OLYMPIC, the invasion of Kyushu set for November 1945, and for Operation CORONET, the crowning blow, the invasion of Honshu and the attack on the Tokyo plain, the following March 1946. With the example of the resistance the Japanese had already put up on the Pacific islands before them, Allied planners sombrely anticipated Allied casualties of over a million for OLYMPIC alone.

Halsey now commanded the most powerful fleet in naval history. Task Force 38, deployed in three task groups, had ten fleet and six light carriers, mounting 1,191 aircraft, eight battleships, nineteen cruisers and over sixty destroyers. This huge striking force began operations off the Japanese mainland on 10 July, with exploratory strikes against airfields on the Tokyo plain. The fleet's tasks were now to reduce the Japanese naval and Army air forces; to attack strategic targets on the Japanese mainland; and to test the strength of Japanese defences in northern Honshu and in Hokkaido, which were both beyond normal reconnaissance range for aircraft from the Marianas (the areas could have been covered by B-29s from Okinawa, but the first operational B-29 sortie over Japan did not take place until the evening before the end of the war). During the coming operations, the Third Fleet's tasks were amended to include the destruction of the remnants of the Japanese Navy and merchant fleet—possibly because Nimitz's staff knew that Halsey would go for Japanese shipping anyway, whether programmed or not.

TF 38 was joined on 16 July, some 300 miles east of Japan, by TF 37, the British Pacific Fleet, with four carriers and 255 aircraft, the battleship *King George V*, six cruisers and fifteen destroyers. Admiral King had once stipulated that the B.P.F. should be at

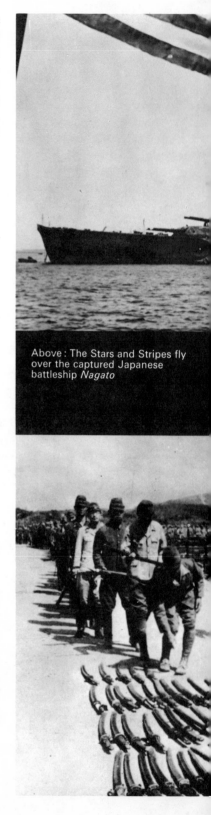

Above: The Stars and Stripes fly over the captured Japanese battleship *Nagato*

Below : Japanese officers surrendering their swords at Kuala Lumpur, October 1945

seven days' notice to join MacArthur's South-west Pacific Area, but this stipulation was long forgotten and the B.P.F. took up an honoured position on the right of TF 38's line.

The operations which the combined carrier fleets were now to carry out were the most finished professional aerial performances of the war at sea—and hence, of all time, for those conditions will never arise again. 'This was the consummation of the carrier art. The great fleet turned and wheeled as one, concentrating to strike, dispersing to fuel, shuttling up and down the coast of Japan at will, advancing and retreating as one great supple weapon.'[27] Halsey was able to call on a varied arsenal of weapons: air strikes, with guns, bombs and torpedoes, battleship and cruiser bombardments (in which the Royal Navy ships joined), surface sweeps by cruisers and destroyers, radio deception, submarine operations, and mining by sea and air.

The Japanese opposition at sea was nonexistent and in the air surprisingly light. The Japanese were once again hoarding their strength against the moment the Allies set foot on Japanese soil. The Allies' main adversary was the weather, which prevented or curtailed flying operations on several days. TF 38 carried out thirteen strike days (TF 37 did eight) and three battleship bombardments. They destroyed or damaged 2,408 aircraft (TF 37 destroyed 347) and sank or damaged 924,000 tons of Japanese shipping (TF 37: 356,760 tons).

Halsey's strikes ranged from Muroran in Hokkaido in the north, all down the coast of Japan to Matsuyama in Shikoku in the south, while his attendant train of fast large tankers and store ships gave him an astounding mobility which Admiral Fraser could only report to the Admiralty with rueful admiration: 'With easy grace he [Halsey] is striking here one day and there the next, replenishing at sea or returning to harbour as the situation demands. With dogged persistence the British Pacific Fleet is keeping up, and if anything is going to stretch its muscles, these operations will. But it is tied by a string to Australia and much handicapped by its few, small, slow tankers.' In the event, the British Pacific Fleet was stretched too far, and many of its ships were denied what they considered to be their proper place at the end by a shortage of fuel.

The surviving heavy ships of the Japanese Navy were all immobilized for lack of fuel and were lying, heavily camouflaged and relegated to the status of floating anti-aircraft batteries, the battleship *Nagato* at Yokosuka and the rest at Kure, on the Inland Sea. In three days of strikes, TF 38's aircraft sank or badly damaged them all, in a final revenge for Pearl Harbor: *Nagato*, the battleships *Haruna*, *Ise* and *Hyuga*, the carriers *Amagi*, *Katsuragi* and *Ryuho*, the cruisers *Tone*, *Aoba*, *Kitagami*, *Iwate* and *Izumo*, and many other smaller warships. Somewhat ungenerously, the Americans excluded the British air groups from these attacks, allotting them secondary targets elsewhere on those strike days.

Operation SNAPSHOT—the U.S. Third Fleet and the British Pacific Fleet manoeuvring in close company after news reached them of Japan's surrender

Halsey later said that he had reluctantly agreed to his staff's insistence that he should forestall any possible post-war British claim that they had delivered even the least part of the final blows which demolished the remains of Japanese sea-power. But it was a churlish way to treat an ally who had actually declared war against Japan only a few hours after the attack on Pearl Harbor.

With news of the first atomic bomb attack on Hiroshima on 6 August, the men in the fleets metaphorically lifted their heads from the business of war to sniff, for the first time, the faint smell of possible peace. But strikes carried on after the second atomic bomb, and even after hostilities had been declared over, Halsey warned his fleet to stay on their guard, because it was possible that the enemy might still attack: 'Any ex-enemy aircraft attacking the fleet', he signalled, 'is to be shot down in a friendly manner.' It was as well he did so, for the very last kamikazes of the war made their attacks as peace was being proclaimed.

After the war, the fleets were the only large Allied forces immediately available to land in Japan and begin the work of repatriating prisoners of war and post-war rehabilitation. But,

while waiting to take part in the surrender of Japan, the fleets
indulged in some excusable showing off. On 16 August and again
on the 17th, the task groups, three American and one British,
closed until destroyer screens were only one mile apart and
enjoyed themselves in some high-speed manoeuvres in close
company, whilst aircraft overhead took photographs in Operation
SNAPSHOT. On 22 August it was the aircrews' turn, in Operation TINTYPE; over a thousand aircraft massed in the sky at
once, their wings stretching to the horizon; they flew over the
ships, squadron after squadron, dipping and rolling to salute the
thousands of bluejackets waving from the decks below.

On 27 August the Allied ships anchored in Sagami Wan, the
outer part of Tokyo Bay. That evening, the snow-capped cone of
Fujiyama, Japan's sacred mountain, stood out exceptionally
clearly against the western sky. 'As evening drew on, the watchers
on the quarterdeck of the *King George V* saw the red orb of the sun
go down right into the middle of the volcano's crater. Rarely, if
ever, can a heavenly body have appeared to act with such
appropriate symbolism.'[28]

Notes

1. Admiral Sir Bruce Fraser, C.-in-C., British Pacific Fleet's Report of Proceedings, 1945.
2. Quoted in S. E. Morison, *History of United States Naval Operations in World War II*, vol. 3, 'The Rising Sun in the Pacific' (Oxford University Press, Oxford and Little, Brown and Co., Boston 1947–59), 15 vols.
3. J. K. Taussig, Jr, 'My Crew at Pearl Harbor', *Esquire* Magazine, March 1943.
4. Lieutenant Commander Howell M. Forgy, Ch.C., '. . . And Pass The Ammunition', Jack S. McDowell (ed.) (Appleton-Century, New York 1944)
5. Forgy, op. cit.
6. Winston S. Churchill, *The Second World War*, vol. 3, 'The Grand Alliance' (Cassell, London and Houghton Mifflin Co., Boston 1948–54), 6 vols.
7. Quoted in Morison, op. cit.
8. Morison, op. cit.
9. Captain Donald MacIntyre, *Fighting Admiral* (Evans Bros., London and British Book Service, Toronto, 1961).
10. MacIntyre, op. cit.
11. MacIntyre, op. cit.
12. Robert J. Casey, *Torpedo Junction: with the Pacific Fleet from Pearl Harbor through Midway* (Bobbs-Merrill Co. Inc., Indianapolis 1943 and Jarrolds, London 1944).
13. Fleet Admiral William F. Halsey U.S.N. and J. Bryan III, *Admiral Halsey's Story* (Whittlesey House, McGraw-Hill Book Co., New York 1947)
14. Quoted in Morison, op. cit., vol. 4, 'Coral Sea, Midway and Submarine Operations'.
15. Lieutenant Clarence E. Dickinson and Boyden Sparkes, *The Flying Guns: the cockpit record of a naval pilot from Pearl Harbor through Midway* (Charles Scribner's Sons, New York 1942).
16. Lieutenant C. G. Morris and Hugh B. Cave, 'I Saw the *Helena* Go Down', *Saturday Evening Post*, 22 January 1944.
17. Robert Sherrod, *Tarawa* (Duell, Sloan and Pearce Inc., New York 1944).
18. Quoted in Morison, op. cit., vol. 7, 'Aleutians, Gilberts and Marshalls'.
19. Quoted in Morison, op. cit.
20. Halsey, op. cit.
21. Halsey, op. cit.
22. Richard Hough, *The Hunting of Force Z* (Collins, London 1963). Published in America under the title *Death of the Battleship* by the Macmillan Co., New York 1963.
23. Georges Blond, 'Le Survivant du Pacifique', from *The Sun Goes Down: last letters from Japanese suicide pilots and soldiers*, Jean Lartéguy (ed.) (William Kimber, London and Ryerson Press, Toronto 1956).
24. John Winton, *The Forgotten Fleet* (Michael Joseph, London 1969 and Coward, McCann and Geoghegan, Inc., New York 1970).
25. Roy E. Appleman, James M. Burns, Russell A. Gugler and John Stevens, *United States Army in World War Two: War in the Pacific, Okinawa, Last Battle* (Historical Division, Department of the Army, Washington 1948).
26. Lartéguy, op. cit.
27. John Winton, *Air Power at Sea: 1939–45* (Sidgwick and Jackson, London 1976 and Thomas Y. Crowell Co. Inc., New York 1977).
28. Captain S. W. Roskill, D.S.C., R.N., *The War at Sea 1939–45* Vol. 3, part 2 (Her Majesty's Stationery Office, London 1961).

Photo Acknowledgements

The publishers and author are grateful to the following for permission to reproduce and for supplying the illustrations on: page 11 *top*, Associated Press; 28 *top right* (IWM), 74 *inset*, 92 *btm*, 185, Camera Press; 13 *centre*, 13 *btm*, Robert Hunt Library; 1 *btm*, 2-3, 9, 24, 31 *top*, 31 *btm*, 34 *left*, 34-5 *centre*, 35 *rt*, 43 *top*, 85, 96, 98 *top*, 98-9 *btm*, 104, 108-9, 111 *btm*, 120, 132-3, 138-9 *btm*, 146, 148-9 *top*, 148-9 *btm*, 150 *left*, 150-1 *centre top*, 151 *top rt*, 154, 156-7, 174-5 *btm*, 178-9 *top*, 178-9 *btm*, 184 *top*, 184 *btm*, 188, 189, Imperial War Museum; 17, 20-1, 26-7, 28 *top left*, 28 *btm*, 32-3, 66, 70 *btm*, 72-3 *top*, 72-3 *btm*, 92 *top left*, 93 *btm*, 95 *top*, 95 *btm*, 100 *top left*, 100 *top rt*, 100 *btm*, 101 *top and btm*, 102, 107 *btm*, 110 *btm*, 110-11 *top*, 112-13, 116 *top*, 117 *top*, 117 *btm*, 119, 122, 125 *rt*, 125 *btm*, 135, 136-7, 150-1 *btm*, 164, 168, 170 *top left*, 170-1 *top centre*, 180, 181, rear endpapers, Keystone Press Agency; 1 *top*, 13 *top*, 54, 84, 92-3 *top centre*, 116 *btm*, 141, 160-1 *top*, 170-1 *btm*, 171 *top rt*, John MacClancy; front endpapers, John MacClancy/US Air Force; 10-11, 14, 16, 18-19 *top*, 42 *top*, 74-5, 108 *left*, 131, 142-3, 144-5 *btm*, 152, 166, John MacClancy/US Navy; 139 *top*, Jennifer Moore Personality Picture Library/US Navy; 6-7, 18-19 *btm*, 36, 39, 40-1 *top and btm*, 42-3 *btm*, 44, 47 *top*, 46-7 *btm*, 48-9, 50-1, 52-3, 56-7, 59, 60-1, 62 *top*, 62 *btm*, 63 *top and btm*, 65 *top and btm*, 69, 76-7, 115 *top and btm*, 144 *top*, 145 *top*, 160 *btm*, 161 *btm*, 163, 172-3, 176, J. G. Moore Collection/US Navy; 22, 46, 82, 87, 90-1, 93 *top rt*, 125 *top left*, 129 *top and btm*, 169, 174-5 *top*, 182, 186-7 *top*, 186-7 *btm*, Popperfoto; 70 *top*, 78, 107 *top*, U.S. Navy.

General Index

Index of Ships